Marketing Organization Development Consulting
A How-To Guide for OD Consultants

Marketing Organization Development Consulting

A How-To Guide for OD Consultants

Edited by
William J. Rothwell
Jong Gyu Park
Jae Young Lee

CRC Press

Taylor & Francis Group
Boca Raton London New York

CRC Press is an imprint of the
Taylor & Francis Group, an **informa** business

A PRODUCTIVITY PRESS BOOK

CRC Press
Taylor & Francis Group
6000 Broken Sound Parkway NW, Suite 300
Boca Raton, FL 33487-2742

Printed on acid-free paper
Version Date: 20161022

International Standard Book Number-13: 978-1-138-03331-3 (Paperback)

Library of Congress Cataloging-in-Publication Data

Names: Rothwell, William J., 1951- author. | Park, Jong Gyu, author. | Yi, Chae-yæong, 1964-, author.
Title: Marketing organization development consulting : a how-to guide for OD consultants /
William J. Rothwell, Jong Gyu Park, Jae Young Lee.
Description: Boca Raton, FL : CRC Press, [2017]
Identifiers: LCCN 2016041202| ISBN 9781138033313 (pbk. : alk. paper) | ISBN 9781315311739 (ebook)
Subjects: LCSH: Consulting firms--Marketing. | Organizational change.
Classification: LCC HD69.C6 R68 2017 | DDC 001--dc23
LC record available at https://lccn.loc.gov/2016041202

Visit the Taylor & Francis Web site at
http://www.taylorandfrancis.com

and the CRC Press Web site at
http://www.crcpress.com

William J. Rothwell dedicates this book to his wife, Marcelina V. Rothwell. She is the wind beneath his wings.

Jong Gyu Park dedicates this book to his wife Bora Kwon and his son Seonjae Park.

Jae Young Lee dedicates this book to her husband, Sewon Song.

Contents

Preface...ix

Acknowledgments xv

Editors..xvii

Contributors xxi

Advance Organizer xxv

1   Unique Challenges in Marketing Change Management,
    Performance Consulting, and Organization Development 1
    WILLIAM J. ROTHWELL

2   Marketing Landscape, Tools, and Definitions...........................13
    MICHELE C. WELLIVER

3   Evaluating Personal Strengths and Weaknesses:
    A Competency-Based Approach 31
    JONG GYU PARK

4   Evaluating Unmet Needs and Opportunities 51
    MARIE CARASCO-SAUL

5   Proposal Process 71
    AILEEN G. ZABALLERO

6   Pricing OD Consulting Services 91
    WILLIAM J. ROTHWELL

7   Channels for OD Marketing...103
    ZAKIYA ALSADAH

8   Communication Planning and Branding 123
    AZADEH OMRANI-KERMANI

9   Personal Sales 133
    JAMIE CAMPBELL

10 **Executive-Level Communications**...159
JAE YOUNG LEE

11 **How Measurement and Appraisal Can Be the Means
to the End of Marketing OD** 173
PATRICIA MACKO

12 **The Future of Marketing OD Consulting**..............................189
WILLIAM J. ROTHWELL

Index 197

Preface

Almost everyone is familiar with the role of a consultant. Above all else, a consultant helps others. But many managers expect the consultant to play medical doctor.

Medical doctors play a helping role, to be sure. Patients go to a physician with pain or other symptoms. The physician, trained in diagnostic methods and a diagnostic protocol, typically begins by asking questions about signs and symptoms causing pain. When sufficient information has been obtained in that fashion, the physician moves on to a physical exam and then more intrusive examinations. The diagnostic approach finds the *root cause(s)*— what is causing the pain—and only then can the physician prescribe medicine or therapy to alleviate pain or address other signs and symptoms.

In the consulting field, many clients expect consultants to behave as physicians do. Consultants are expected to ask questions, gather information, and make recommendations to solve problems. The consultant plays the expert and gives the client an answer. It is then up to the client to implement the course of treatment sufficient to solve the problem.

The problem with the expert (medical doctor) approach to diagnosis is that it assumes that the consultant is the expert and the client needs treatment. Its focus is always on what is wrong and what causes pain. It builds up the credibility of the consultant at the expense of the client's ownership in change. Clients have no ownership in the problems, solutions, action plans, or metrics identified by the consultant because they do not understand how consultants arrived at the conclusions and recommendations. More often than not, external expert consultants' recommendations are rejected because the client has no buy-in to what the expert believes. That leaves a bad impression in the minds of clients in working with consultants.

But there is another way. It is the approach used by person-centered clinical psychologists. That approach differs completely from the medical doctor approach.

Clinical psychologists assume that clients already know their problems, already have good ideas about how to solve the problems, but for some reason are not implementing the solution(s). The psychologist's role is to help clients identify the barriers that keep them from implementing their own solutions and knock down those barriers.

Organization development (OD) consultants function like person-centered clinical psychologists. OD consultants assume that the people inside an organization are actually the best experts on what problems face the organization, what causes those problems, how important those problems are, what solutions should address the problems, how those solutions should be measured, and how those solutions should be implemented. The real problem for OD consultants is that the members of the organization do not agree among themselves about their problems, what causes those problems, how important it is to solve them, how to solve them, how to measure the success of solution implementation, or how to implement the solutions. The challenge is herding cats to a common goal. It is a matter of facilitating the change rather than imposing it based on expert knowledge.

In the OD field, one big challenge is overcoming the assumption of managers and other stakeholders that the consultant is the expert, a "doctor" who always has "medicine." While there may be comfort to be gained by assuming that other people always have solutions to our problems, it is not an effective assumption in the long term. It will not stick because people do not buy in. Nor does solving other people's problems lead those people to take responsibility or learn how to solve their own problems.

It is this assumption that consultants are always experts that leads to marketing challenges for OD consultants. Everyone wants someone else to tell them what to do. Once they are told, they reject it and then blame the consultant. Much time, money, and effort are then wasted in a fruitless search to have experts solve problems. When consultants succeed and find recommended solutions, many clients refuse to believe them.

So, how do OD consultants market their services when clients expect them to behave in ways they have been trained not to behave? Therein is the marketing dilemma. This book is about how to overcome that dilemma by finding effective marketing strategies for a different approach to consulting.

Audience for This Book

This book is for current or aspiring OD consultants and managers who wish to apply facilitative approaches to change. It addresses the marketing issues affecting both those who work inside organizations (that is, internal OD consultants) and those who work outside organizations (that is, external consultants). It should also interest others, such as human resource professionals and operating managers, who have reason to manage change in organizational settings and to market or sell that change.

Overview of the Contents

This book comprises 12 chapters. The guiding framework of the book is an implicit model of marketing.

Chapter 1 is entitled "Unique Challenges in Marketing Change Management, Performance Consulting, and Organization Development." It defines these special terms and briefly describes the histories of each field, emphasizing how these approaches to consulting differ and why that is important to marketing.

Chapter 2 reviews important marketing terms and popular tools used in the marketing process. This chapter also outlines the many roles a consultant must fill in order to successfully get and keep business (i.e., marketer, salesman, brand manager, account manager) and then discusses the unique differences between marketing OD and marketing other approaches to consulting. Furthermore, it draws a distinction between marketing challenges for internal and external consultants.

Chapter 3 describes the criteria of self-evaluation as an OD consultant. It examines how to identify your strengths and the competencies you need to develop based on OD competencies. This chapter discusses the various consulting styles and how one needs to flexibly adapt his or her personal style to the role that the client demands. Also covered are what a capability statement is, what components it should include, and some tips on how to develop an effective capability statement.

Chapter 4 describes determining needs and opportunities about the market. It provides an introduction to actionable steps and resources for OD, change management, and performance management consultants to evaluate unmet needs and opportunities through a niche market for consulting services. The chapter will also cover how to identify a niche market and how to develop strategy for OD marketing.

Chapter 5 discusses the basics of the request for proposal (RFP) and key aspects to consider about the client when writing a proposal. This chapter further differentiates OD consulting and management consulting and how the proposal reflects the difference, as well as distinguish the difference between work as a contractor/vendor, freelancer, or consultant. In addition, this includes discussing the financial considerations when OD consultants prepare the proposal.

Chapter 6 examines pricing consulting services in OD. It examines such issues as the following: what are common pricing situations in consulting, what makes the pricing of OD consulting services different from pricing in management or performance consulting, and what philosophical issues should be addressed by OD consultants as they consider their pricing strategies for their work and for their clients.

Chapter 7 describes various channels of OD marketing such as viral, word of mouth, and social media marketing. This is important because much business in external consulting work is driven by this marketing. This chapter describes and illustrates through examples the power of viral marketing and social media and how it's used to sell your services.

Chapter 8 covers how to communicate value to your target customers and how to brand your service. This chapter also includes how to differentiate yourself from the competition and brand your consulting service(s). Integral to marketing is developing a marketing communication plan. Here, we discuss creating a plan to direct your marketing efforts. This includes discussing the process of communication, channels to get access to your market, and setting clear objectives of your marketing efforts.

Chapter 9 reviews how to sell your consulting service. This chapter discusses the importance of having a defined sales process to which you adhere. Covered are the steps in the sales process using a sales funnel approach to visualize the process. In addition, this chapter also covers presentation skills, elevator pitches, lead generation, and cold calling. An elevator pitch is especially important for the internal consultant because opportunities may present themselves during their normal day to get buy-in from their coworkers or managers.

Chapter 10 discusses executive communication and getting past the gatekeeper, chief executive officers, and board members. In addition, we discuss how to get past the gatekeepers and get to the financial buyers and decision makers in a company. Techniques for both internal and external consultants are included.

Chapter 11 discusses different way to use common evaluation methods to prove value for performance management, change management, or OD consulting services. The chapter covers return on investment, discounted cash flow, net present value, cost of capital, and hurdle rate. Then we explain how these metrics are used by many companies and how you can use them to sell your services.

Chapter 12 discusses the future. What is the future of marketing for OD? We offer some predictions about the future of marketing OD.

Acknowledgments

The editors thank the many people who helped make this book possible. That includes chapter authors as well as those who reviewed the manuscript to improve it.

Of special note, we would like to thank Jae Young Lee for her help in finding and checking any necessary copyright permissions and Alexandria Gryder for looking over the manuscript and suggesting improvements.

Editors

William J. Rothwell is president of Rothwell & Associates, Inc., and Rothwell & Associates, LLC (see www.rothwellandassociates.com). He is also a professor in the Workforce Education and Development program, Department of Learning and Performance Systems, at The Pennsylvania State University, University Park campus. He has authored, coauthored, edited, or coedited 300 books, book chapters, and articles—including more than 90 books.

Before arriving at Penn State in 1993, he had 20 years of work experience as a training director, human resources, and organization development specialist in government and in business. He has also worked as a consultant for more than 40 multinational corporations, including Motorola China, General Motors, Ford, and many others. In 2012 he earned American Society of Training and Development's (ASTD) prestigious Distinguished Contribution to Workplace Learning and Performance Award, and in 2013, ASTD honored him by naming him as a Certified Professional in Learning and Performance (CPLP) Fellow. In 2014, he was given the Asia-Pacific International Personality Brandlaureate Award (see http://www.thebrandlaureate .com/awards/ibp_bpa.php).

Truly global in his outlook, he conducted training in 15 nations around the globe in 2014 alone and visited many other nations virtually to offer webinars. Notably, in 2015, he visited China for his 76th time since 1996.

His recent books include *Organization Development Fundamentals: Managing Strategic Change* (ATD Press, 2015), *The Competency Toolkit*, 2 volumes, 2nd ed. (HRD Press, 2015), *Creating Engaged Employees: It's Worth the Investment* (ATD Press, 2014), *The Leader's Daily Role in Talent Management: Maximizing Results, Engagement and Retention* (Institute for Training and Development [Malaysia], 2014), *Optimizing Talent in the Federal Workforce* (Management Concepts, 2014), *Performance Consulting*

(Wiley, 2014), the *ASTD Competency Study: The Training and Development Profession Redefined* (ASTD, 2013), *Becoming an Effective Mentoring Leader: Proven Strategies for Building Excellence in Your Organization* (McGraw-Hill, 2013), *Talent Management: A Step-by-Step Action-Oriented Approach Based on Best Practice* (HRD Press, 2012), the edited three-volume *Encyclopedia of Human Resource Management* (Wiley/Pfeiffer, 2012), *Lean but Agile: Rethink Workforce Planning and Gain a True Competitive Advantage* (Amacom, 2012), *Invaluable Knowledge: Securing Your Company's Technical Expertise—Recruiting and Retaining Top Talent, Transferring Technical Knowledge, Engaging High Performers* (Amacom, 2011), *Competency-Based Training Basics* (ASTD Press, 2010), *Effective Succession Planning: Ensuring Leadership Continuity and Building Talent from Within*, 4th ed. (Amacom, 2010), *Practicing Organization Development*, 3rd ed. (Pfeiffer, 2009), *Basics of Adult Learning* (ASTD, 2009), *HR Transformation* (Davies-Black, 2008), *Working Longer: New Strategies for Managing, Training, and Retaining Older Employees* (Amacom, 2008), and *Cases in Government Succession Planning: Action—Oriented Strategies for Public-Sector Human Capital Management, Workforce Planning, Succession Planning, and Talent Management* (HRD Press, 2008). He can be reached by e-mail at wjr9@psu.edu and by phone at 814-863-2581.

Jong Gyu Park is a senior partner of Rothwell & Associates, LLC. He specializes in the areas of human resource management (HRM) and organization development (OD). Prior to working at Rothwell & Associates, LLC, he was a management consultant at Deloitte and Talent & Rewards Group of Willis Towers Watson, where he managed and administered various HRM and OD consulting projects.

He has worked with both domestic clients in South Korea and multinational clients in a number of different industries. A partial list of clients includes Allianz Life Insurance, Hyundai-Kia Motors, ATD, Halogen, ING Life, Korea Exchange Bank, LG Corp., Ministry of Environment, Ministry of Strategy and Finance, and SK Corp., etc.

He earned his PhD in business administration with an emphasis on management at the Sungkyunkwan University in Seoul, South Korea. He is a PhD candidate in Workforce Education & Development with an emphasis on organization development at The Pennsylvania State University. He can be reached at JGP@RothwellandAssociates.com.

Jae Young Lee is a PhD candidate in the Workforce Education and Development program with an emphasis in human resource development (HRD) and organization development (OD) at The Pennsylvania State University. She earned a BA and an MEd in Educational Technology, and both degrees were earned at Ewha Woman's University in South Korea.

Her career encompasses human resource development, human resource management, and global business. She worked at KT&G, the fifth biggest tobacco company in the world, for a decade as an HRD manager at the HRD, and the human resource (HR) manager at the global business department.

Her research interests include strategic HRD, OD, employee engagement, leadership, and self-directed learning.

Contributors

Zakiya Alsadah is from Saudi Arabia and is a doctoral candidate in the Department of Learning and Performance Systems at Penn State. Her focus is organization development and human resources development. Her research interest is in the talent development/work engagement. She earned a BS degree in biology from Saudi Arabia and a certificate in English from the IECP Institute at Penn State. She has worked as a volunteer English teacher. Zakiya completed her master's from Penn State in Workforce Education and Development with a focus in communication in multicultural workplaces. She decided to broaden her insights into the importance of an organization's human resources, which fueled the desire to pursue a PhD degree.

Jamie Campbell has been devoted to working with students from various backgrounds for over a decade. Through his leadership, Jamie has successfully developed scholarship and summer programs for Project Grad Atlanta and managed student organizations at Morehouse College. With aggressive fundraising and ethical management of budgetary requirements, Jamie has helped to implement and create diversity enhancement programs at The Pennsylvania State University.

Jamie is the 2013 Dr. James Robinson Equal Opportunity Award winner. This award is given to recognize a Penn State faculty or staff member who has contributed to the university by improving cross-cultural understanding. He was also recognized as a finalist for The Advisor of the Year Award at The Pennsylvania State University. He has served as a panelist on topics ranging from social justice to students' issues and has served as a speaker for several leadership programs. Jamie also serves as an advisor to several student organizations within the Smeal College of Business and continues to mentor graduates working in Fortune 500 companies.

Currently, Jamie is the assistant dean for Diversity Enhancement Programs at the Smeal College of Business. He is a 1995 graduate of Morehouse College, where he earned his BA in sociology and was inducted into Alpha Kappa Delta (national honor society for sociology). He earned his ME with concentrations in adult education and instruction education from Central Michigan University in 2003. During his matriculation at Central Michigan University, he was selected for admission into Phi Delta Kappa (national honor society for education). Jamie is currently a PhD candidate in the Workforce Education Program at The Pennsylvania State University. He and his wife Kimberly are the parents of three children (Grace, Vivian, and Lillian).

Marie Carasco-Saul is the managing director of Talent en Floré Ltd. Co. She is a high-potential talent thought leader with expertise in organization diagnosis and conflict management. As a millennial and mid-career professional coach, Marie advises leadership teams and individuals to strategically manage talent, navigate career decisions respectively, and address issues with interpersonal workplace dynamics.

Marie has worked both in the United States and United Kingdom at three headquarter locations supporting global talent management and change initiatives of the world's largest oilfield service organization with responsibilities in North America, Singapore, Malaysia, Russia, France, and the continent of Africa. She has over 10 years of combined experience in career development, human resource management, conflict resolution, and training.

In 2014, she and her coauthors were awarded the prestigious Cutting Edge Award by the Academy of Human Resource Development for her research on leadership and employee engagement.

Marie earned a PhD in workforce education and development with an emphasis in human resource development and organization development from The Pennsylvania State University. She is an executive MBA candidate at the University of Texas–Dallas Naveen Jindal School of Management. She earned an undergraduate degree in psychology and a graduate degree in industrial–organizational psychology. You can reach her at marie@talentenflore.com.

Patricia Macko is a third-year PhD candidate in the Workforce Education and Development program with an emphasis in human resource development/organization development. Her dissertation will focus on integrated talent development. She has 20 years of experience in the financial services industry, specifically in the areas of training and development, human resource management, business development, and sales. She has earned a BS in business administration and an MS in instructional technology. She also earned the designation of Certified Credit Union Executive.

For a decade, she held a senior leadership position with Belco Community Credit Union in Harrisburg, Pennsylvania. Her most recent position with Belco was training director. As training director, Patricia was responsible for setting the strategic direction for the training and development of all employees. Several of her accomplishments while working for Belco were the development and oversight of a formal human resource and training department, creation and facilitation of a strategic planning process, development of a formal succession planning process, development of a sales force and sales culture, and the research, development, and implementation of a formal human resource development planning process. Pat's expertise includes project management, strategic planning, organization development, talent development, human resource management, and performance improvement.

Azadeh Omrani-Kermani is a global professional as an organization development consultant. Her focus is on human resource management, team building, leadership, and entrepreneurship. She works as an entrepreneur and business development consultant and designs workshops for both new enterprises and corporations on how to develop their business model, digital communication, and leadership. She is an expert in organization development, along with personal development to facilitate leadership, communication skills, and team building strategies.

She has four years of experience in consulting information technology companies and four years of experience working at the Chamber of Commerce in Iran as a researcher and export marketing consultant. She had held a position as executive officer of the private and public council and provides research on facilitating private sector trade through regulations. She has also consulted hundreds of small- and medium-sized enterprises, aiding them in defining and establishing business strategies and export marketing plans to expand overseas markets through the Chamber of Commerce. Azadeh earned an undergraduate degree in mathematics and master's degrees in business administration and strategic communications. You can reach her at kermani.azadeh@gmail.com.

Michele C. Welliver is a PhD candidate in the Workforce Education and Development program with an emphasis in human resource development and organization development at The Pennsylvania State University. Her teaching and research interests are in sales and marketing. She earned a BA in mass communications and advertising from Bloomsburg University of Pennsylvania and an MBA in marketing from Wilkes University of Pennsylvania. She also earned the American Marketing Association's Professional Certified Marketer (PCM) certification.

Michele has been a marketing instructor at Bloomsburg University for the past 18 years and is currently the Frederick Douglass Teaching Scholar for the Department of Management and Marketing. She has also served as a faculty advisor and coach for both undergraduate and graduate students at the annual National Collegiate Sales Competition at Kennesaw State University and the Retail Collegiate Challenge at Kutztown University.

In addition to her teaching experience, she enjoyed a rewarding career in media sales, where she developed and managed new, direct revenue radio accounts and created and implemented marketing campaigns for radio advertisers. She worked as a director of marketing and research in the broadcast industry directing station marketing initiatives, including strategic planning, community service campaigns, and public relations support. She also developed nontraditional revenue projects and supervised station research projects encompassing both the news and sales departments.

Aileen G. Zaballero is a senior partner for R&A and a dual-title PhD candidate in workforce education and development and comparative international education, with an emphasis on organization development, at The Pennsylvania State University. She has been a certified professional in learning and performance (CPLP) through ATD (formerly ASTD) since 2009. Her research focuses on the human factors and group processes that influence the competitive performance of businesses. Her recent publications include chapters in *Performance Consulting* (John Wiley & Sons, 2013), *Optimizing Talent in the Federal Workforce* (Management Concepts, 2014), *The Competency Toolkit, 2nd ed.* (HRD Press, 2014), *Encyclopedia of Human Resource Management, Vol. 2* (Pfeiffer, 2012), and *Handbook of Research on Workforce Diversity in a Global Society* (IGI Global, 2012).

Advance Organizer

William J. Rothwell

Complete the following Organizer before you read the book. Use it as a diagnostic tool to help you assess what you most want to know about marketing organization development (OD) consulting—and where you can find it in this book *fast*.

The Organizer

Directions

Read each item in the following Organizer. Circle a *True* (*T*), a *Not Applicable* (*N/A*), or *False* (*F*) in the left column opposite each item. Spend about 10 minutes on the Organizer. Be honest! Think of marketing OD as you would like it to be—not what some expert says it is. When you finish, score and interpret the results using the instructions appearing at the end of the Organizer. Then be prepared to share your responses with others you know to help you think about what you most want to learn about OD marketing. If you would like to learn more about one item below, refer to the number in the right column to find the chapter in this book in which the subject is discussed.

The Questions

Circle your response for each item below:		OD consultants should:	Chapter in the book in which the topic is covered:
T N/A F	1.	Be familiar with unique challenges in marketing change management, performance consulting, and organization development	1
T N/A F	2.	Be familiar with the basic principles of traditional marketing	2
T N/A F	3.	Be able to identify personal strengths and weaknesses	3
T N/A F	4.	Know how to evaluate unmet client needs and opportunities	4
T N/A F	5.	Be able to write an effective proposal	5
T N/A F	6.	Create pricing strategy for OD consulting	6
T N/A F	7.	Identify channels for OD marketing	7
T N/A F	8.	Build a personal brand as a consultant	8
T N/A F	9.	Engage in "personal selling"	9
T N/A F	10.	Communicate effectively with executives	10
T N/A F	11.	Measure the effectiveness of OD marketing efforts	11
T N/A F	12.	Describe ideas for future OD marketing efforts	12
____ Total			

Scoring and Interpreting the Organizer

Give yourself *1 point for each T* and a *0 for each F or N/A* listed above. Total the points from the *T* column and place the sum in the line opposite to the word TOTAL above. Then interpret your score as follows:

Score

11–12 points	=	Congratulations! Give yourself a grade of A. You may be doing an effective job of marketing OD services and OD consulting.
9–10 points	=	Give yourself a grade of B. You are doing many things right in marketing OD services and OD consulting. But there is room for improvement. Note those. Focus your attention on those.
7–8 points	=	Give yourself a grade of C. You are muddling through. You should focus on improving how you market OD services and OD consulting.
5–6 points	=	Give yourself a grade of D. You are below average in marketing OD services and OD consulting. Act to improve your marketing!
4–0 points	=	Give yourself a grade of F. You are failing in marketing OD services and OD consulting. *Take immediate action to improve!*

Chapter 1

Unique Challenges in Marketing Change Management, Performance Consulting, and Organization Development

William J. Rothwell

Contents

What Is Change Management?...2
What Is Performance Consulting?...3
What Is OD?..6
What Do Change Management, Performance Consulting,
and OD Share in Common?..8
Why Is Marketing Important to Change Management, Performance
Consulting, and OD? 9
Summary..10
References 11

What is change management? What is performance consulting? What is organization development (OD)? What do these fields share in common? What does marketing these three types of consulting services share in common? Why is marketing important for all of them? This introductory chapter answers these fundamental questions.

What Is Change Management?

It is worth stating at the outset of any discussion on change management that experts do not agree among themselves on definitions, conceptual frameworks, or other characteristics of change management.

But for this chapter, let's accept the definition of change management used by the Association of Change Management Professionals (ACMP). They say it is "a deliberate set of activities that facilitate and support the success of individual and organizational change and the realization of its intended business results" (see http://www.acmpglobal.org/?page=WhatisCM). It is worthy of note that the ACMP has published organizational standards to guide effective organizational change efforts (see http://www.acmpglobal .org/?TheStandard).

Many change management professionals are steeped in project management approaches. They emphasize those. While there is nothing wrong with doing that, and it leads to well-organized change efforts in organizational settings, the real question amounts to this: in a change effort, what is more important—the project plan or the people going through the change? For some in the change management field, the project plan takes priority. People—their feelings, beliefs, values, and aspirations—are secondary.

Change management is often driven by models that simplify project planning. Many such models are well known. An example of such a model is John Kotter's model, which lists the desirable stages in change management. The stages in the most recent version of the model, as described on Kotter's website at http://www.kotterinternational.com/the-8-step-process-for-leading -change/, are to

- Create a sense of urgency
- Build a guiding coalition
- Form a strategic vision and initiatives
- Enlist a volunteer army
- Enable action by removing barriers
- Generate short-term wins
- Sustain acceleration
- Institute change

Note that this is a generic model, suitable for driving any change effort. It does not matter if the change focuses on a new product launch, a new employee benefit program, a new software program implementation, or some other change. These general steps can drive a more detailed, task-focused project plan.

Kotter's model is based on research of successful change efforts. Even if it is not accepted and some other is used, Kotter's steps provide useful criteria against which to judge the effectiveness of a change effort. If the issues covered in Kotter's model are addressed by some other model, then it is more likely to be aligned with the success factors shared by many organizational change efforts across many industries and national cultures.

Many other well-known change models exist. Many such models are described on this website: http://www.change-management-coach.com/change -management-models.html.

What Is Performance Consulting?

Performance consulting goes by many names. Some call it human performance technology; some call it human performance improvement; some call it human performance engineering; and some call it human performance enhancement. Despite these many names, the approach applies a systematic, problem-solving approach to addressing human productivity problems.

Performance is understood to mean work results (outputs) and the behaviors associated with getting the results. Other elements can be added to this common understanding of performance. For instance, it may be possible to add values (a continuum ranging from what the people of the organization regard as important to not important) and ethics (a continuum ranging from what people of the organization regard as right and wrong).

Performance consulting is associated with systematically analyzing problems with human productivity and finding the best, most cost-effective and ethically justifiable solutions to those problems. It is sometimes confused with *performance management*, which is helping people achieve results in organizational settings. In recent years, performance consulting has also focused on finding organizational and individual strengths (and solving problems with human beings in organizational contexts) and leveraging those strengths to competitive advantage.

Performance consultants often—but we cannot say "always"—approach problems with human productivity in the same way as medical doctors diagnose illnesses with the human body (see Rothwell, 2000, 2015b; Rothwell, Benscoter, Zaballero, Park, Kim, & Kim, 2014; Rothwell, Hohne & King, 2007).

Medical doctors are trained on an approach to diagnosis, and they apply it when confronted by a patient complaining about signs and symptoms of health problems. (A sign is a visible expression of a problem; a symptom results from the underlying root cause of the problem.) Physicians confronted by patients with health problems will usually begin by asking questions to gather background information. They will then move on to physical examinations to be clear on exactly what part(s) of the human anatomy are affected. They will move beyond physical examinations to more intrusive examinations that may require x-rays, magnetic resonance imaging, blood tests, and other such tests. The whole point of medical diagnosis is to eliminate alternative explanations of root causes. Then and only then can physicians prescribe medicine or recommend therapy. To do otherwise is to be guilty of malpractice.

Performance consultants often follow a similar approach. They know that, when confronted with problems with human productivity, managers have not been trained on systematic approaches to diagnose those problems. They will jump to conclusions about what to do—or about what causes the problem. Managers will also confuse signs and symptoms with root causes.

Consider a simple example. A manager has a worker not performing her job effectively. The manager visits the human resource (HR) department, asking for help. The manager may jump to many conclusions. For instance, the manager may assume the employee is lazy, needs training, or needs something else. The manager may then jump from assumptions about causes to solutions. HR managers know that when managers reach their wit's ends with employee problems, they will often go to HR and request training. But training is rarely the correct solution. Training will solve only problems that are caused by lack of knowledge, skill, or attitude. If the performance problem is caused by anything else—such as lack of correct supervision, lack of equipment, lack of feedback, or lack of hundreds or even thousands of other root causes—then training is not the correct, or most cost-effective, solution. The most cost-effective solutions can only be determined when the root cause(s) have been narrowed down.

Many models have been described to guide performance consulting. Some are situation-specific models intended to be used in a certain situation (such as a request for training); some are comprehensive models intended to compare the organization against a more desirable profile (such as Six

Sigma, Lean Manufacturing, or Balridge criteria) or management preferences (such as a vision of a desired future).

Rothwell (2015a) describes a model that can be used both to guide problem solving in situations and comprehensively for troubleshooting problems with individuals, teams, departments, divisions, organizations, industries, communities, or nations. The steps of the model are simple. They require posing, and answering, simple yet profound questions:

1. What is the current situation? (Describe it.)
2. What is the desired situation? (Describe it.)
3. What is the measurable gap between questions 1 and 2?
4. How important is the gap? (Clarify why it is important and to whom it is important.)
5. What causes the gap? (Try to determine underlying causes of the measurable gap.)
6. What range of solutions can close the gap? (Consider possible solutions and their relative costs, advantages, and disadvantages.)
7. What side effects may be experienced for each possible solution? (Doctors know that medicine has side effects. Performance consultants know that any change in an organizational system will have both intended and unintended consequences. What are the likely negative consequences, and how can they be avoided or mitigated?)
8. How can the best solution be chosen and implemented?
9. How can the results be measured? (How well does the implemented solution close the measurable gaps?)

Each step of this model requires interaction with many stakeholders—understood to mean people who care about solutions to problems.

Performance consultants focus on the human side of the enterprise. Broader than that are management consultants, who can focus on—and even specialize in—other issues affecting organizational life. Some management consultants focus on accounting, operations, manufacturing, inventory control, engineering, computer systems, and much more. Conceptually, management consulting is an umbrella term that encompasses all consultants who function in their approach much like medical doctors. Performance consultants specialize on the human side, drawing in other management consultants as needed to deal with broader issues affecting an organization.

What Is OD?

OD is a field of practice that approaches change efforts in a systematic, humanistic way (Rothwell, 2015b; Rothwell, Stavros, & Sullivan, 2015). OD focuses on helping individuals and groups work together interpersonally more effectively. It elevates caring about people over project plans.

OD is often confused with change management and with performance consulting. It is not the same thing. Focusing on human interaction rather than on project results has profound implications for practice. Focusing on human interaction rather than on solving productivity problems also has profound implications for practice.

OD uses a different consulting philosophy than other types of consulting do. While the medical approach is popular and pervasive for consultants, it is not the only role that consultants can play. An alternative, favored by OD, is the psychology approach.

When psychologists are confronted by a patient with a problem, they do not approach the situation as medical doctors approach problems with physical health. Mental health requires a different approach. One issue is that most people are familiar with the medical approach, but fewer people are familiar with how psychologists approach helping situations. One reason is there is a stigma attached to seeking help with psychological problems, and so even those who have experienced psychological treatment may be reluctant to admit it.

When a client approaches a psychologist, the psychologist does not open the discussion as a medical doctor typically does. While a doctor might open with a question like "what seems to be the problem?" (and thereby prompting the client to describe signs and symptoms), a psychologist might open with a broader question like "what brings you to see me today?" The psychologist does not assume there is a problem. Instead, the psychologist knows that the client already knows what issues he or she has and what actions he or she should take. For instance, if the client has an alcohol abuse problem, the client already knows he or she has a drinking problem and already knows what to do to solve the problem—that is, stop drinking. But something is preventing the individual from implementing the solution, and that is why the individual seeks help. The psychologist tries to help the client troubleshoot his or her own problems and overcome whatever barriers prevent successful implementation of solutions leading to improved mental health.

OD consultants follow an approach similar to psychologists of the Carl Rogers' school of Humanistic Psychology. They serve as facilitators, not as experts. They help groups work together more effectively rather than step in to address other issues.

Many psychologists have the luxury of dealing with one person at a time. But OD consultants work with many people. And that creates a challenge. As the old saying goes, "what you see depends on where you sit" (that is, on the organization chart). What the chief executive officer sees is not the same as what the vice president (VP) of HR sees, and what the VP of HR sees is not the same as what a company janitor sees. OD consultants realize that many people in organizational settings possess worthwhile, and useful, knowledge. The goal of OD consultants is to facilitate a process whereby many ideas, from many places, are heard—and used—to solve problems or identify and leverage organizational competitive strengths.

OD, as a label, is much like the brand name of a computer. But it is the chip inside the computer that makes it work. OD is driven by two major change models, which might be regarded as the "chip" inside the "OD computer."

One chip is the Action Research Model (ARM). The oldest and most traditional model guiding the role of consultants, the ARM (which has been described in print in many ways) requires consultants to

- Enter the system to help solve a problem
- Negotiate a relationship with the client
- Gather initial information from many stakeholders
- Feed back and gain agreement on what the problems are
- Gather information from many stakeholders about possible solutions
- Feed back and gain agreement on what the solutions should be
- Gather information from many stakeholders about implementation plans and measures of success
- Feed back and gain agreement on how the solutions should be implemented and evaluated
- Evaluate results during implementation
- Ensure institutionalization of the change effort
- Leave the system

Note that this approach positions people in the organizations as experts. The consultant does not play doctor, playing "answer man" or "decision maker." Instead, the responsibility for the change remains with the workers and managers.

In recent years, an alternative "chip" has grown in popularity. Going by such names as appreciative inquiry or positive change theory, it relies on a slightly different approach (which has been published in many forms). The consultant works with organizational members and stakeholders to

■ Clarify what gives the organization strength
■ Identify key issues that make people proud of the organization and energize them
■ Establish a shared vision of how the best of the organization can be intensified
■ Clarify a shared vision on how to realize the vision/dream of a better future
■ Appraise the benefits of the change on a continuing basis, using it to encourage people in their change effort

What Do Change Management, Performance Consulting, and OD Share in Common?

Change management consultants, performance consultants, and OD consultants share at least one thing in common. They are all consultants! That means they set out to help those they serve and work with.

But consultants do not necessarily share the same philosophy of the consultant's role. Performance consultants "play doctor" in diagnosing productivity problems and finding solutions. They gather information, analyze it, and offer recommendations to improve organizational conditions. That is a familiar approach to many managers.

Change management consultants "play project managers" and help organizational leaders clarify the project plan for a change effort. They focus on getting goals and deadlines clear and getting responsibilities clear. Then they manage against the project targets.

OD consultants "play psychologists." They facilitate problem-solving efforts conducted by all stakeholders. Their goal is to get buy-in and build a culture that sustains a change. Change managers focus on a goal of getting clarity on the implementation plan, while performance consultants focus on getting quick results by taking responsibility to conduct diagnosis and issue recommendations.

Why Is Marketing Important to Change Management, Performance Consulting, and OD?

Consultants cannot help anyone if nobody is aware of what they have to offer. Marketing is all about creating services that people want and need. It is also about communicating to others what those services are and how consultants can help.

But performance consultants, change management consultants, and OD consultants share a similar problem. The problem is that many managers do not know what help these consultants can provide or how they can help.

In the marketing field, there is a term for selling or promoting something that people are unaware of. That term is *unsought good*. It means a product or a service of which people are not aware of.

A simple example of an unsought good comes from the early days of personal computers. At one time, personal computers had little memory. Early machines had 8K or 16K. They were far less powerful than today's computers. A computer with memory that small cannot do much. People said, "why would I want to spend a lot of money on a computer when it can do very little for me, and I would have to spend much time to learn how to use it?" The point is that, in the early days of personal computers, they were classic examples of an unsought good. People were not aware of them, nor could they see their potential compared to typewriters or other more obvious tools for writing letters, creating spreadsheets, or solving complex mathematical problems. In the early days of computers, a big problem that computer manufacturers had to deal with is that people did not know why they wanted to buy a computer.

While performance consulting, change management, and OD have been around for many years, still very many managers have never heard of these terms. These managers have little awareness of how this consulting compares to other types of consulting. Confusion is common. While sophisticated organizations are familiar with these terms and approaches, most organizations in the world are not sophisticated. Managers may not be familiar with the value that can be added by a change management consultant, a performance consultant, or an OD consultant.

To make matters worse, most marketing and sales books focus on tangible consumer goods. And it is actually different to market a refrigerator or an automobile from consulting services. We can open and close the door of a refrigerator and experience its relative coolness; we can test-drive a car to see how it performs. But consulting services are intangible and depend on brand name, track record of performance with other organizations, and reputational position. Consultants specialize in a change effort—and examples of those include types of change efforts (such as mergers, teambuilding events, succession planning) or approaches to change (such as a focus on solving problems or identifying and building on strengths).

Marketing all three consulting approaches requires unique approaches not typically taught in university marketing courses. Consultants must learn to build and sustain a brand reputation, focus on a unique line or lines of business, and target attention on specific needs.

OD consultants face a greater burden. While most people are familiar with the medical model of consulting in which the consultant plays diagnostician and decision maker, fewer are familiar with the psychological model of consulting in which the consultant plays facilitator. When managers hear of it, they may resist the approach by complaining that they can do their own facilitation—most cannot—and that polling stakeholders to identify problems, solutions, and action plans will take too long. In reality, technology makes it possible to poll huge groups to arrive at decisions in real time, but some managers have never seen such an approach in action. The result: resistance from stakeholders about using an OD-related approach.

Summary

This chapter defined change management, performance consulting, and OD consulting. It described what each approach to consulting means and models to guide them. As the chapter explained, all three share in common that they are consulting efforts. Change management consultants elevate project plans over people; OD elevates the people over the project plan; and performance consulting focuses on discovering the root cause(s) of human productivity problems. All three share in common the problem that managers may not be familiar with these approaches and how they may add value to organizational change efforts.

Use the worksheet appearing in Table 1.1 to organize your thinking and do brainstorming.

Table 1.1 A Worksheet to Organize Your Thinking on Marketing Consulting Services

	Directions: Use this Worksheet to organize your thinking on marketing consulting services. For each question appearing in the left column below, provide your own answers in the right column. There are no "right" or "wrong" answers in any absolute sense.	
Questions		*Answers*
1	What unique challenges will consultants face in marketing change management to prospective clients?	
2	What unique challenges will consultants face in marketing performance consulting to prospective clients?	
3	How is OD different from change management?	
4	How is OD different from performance consulting?	
5	What unique challenges will consultants face in marketing OD? How can those challenges be overcome?	

References

Rothwell, W. (2000). *ASTD models for human performance: Roles, competencies, outputs* (2nd ed.). Alexandria, VA: The American Society for Training and Development.

Rothwell, W. (2015a). *Beyond training and development* (3rd ed.). Amherst, MA: HRD Press.

Rothwell, W. (Ed.). (2015b). *Organization development fundamentals: Managing strategic change*. Alexandria, VA: ATD Press.

Rothwell, W., Benscoter, B., Zaballero, A. Park, J. G., Kim, T., & Kim, W. (2014). *Performance consulting: Applying performance improvement in human resource development*. New York: John Wiley.

Rothwell, W., Hohne, C., & King, S. (2007). *Human performance improvement: Building practitioner performance* (2nd ed.). Boston: Butterworth-Heineman (an imprint of Elsevier).

Rothwell, W., Stavros, J., & Sullivan, R. (Eds.). (2015). *Practicing organization development: A guide for leading change* (5th ed.). New York: John Wiley.

Chapter 2

Marketing Landscape, Tools, and Definitions

Michele C. Welliver

Contents

Chapter Overview 14
Marketing Overview 15
  Marketing Defined 15
    Creating Value for Customers 17
    Building Strong Relationships with Customers 17
    Capturing Value in Return from Customers 18
Marketing Services for the OD Consultant 18
  Intangibility 19
  Inconsistency 21
  Inseparability 21
  Inventory 22
The Marketing Process 22
  Step 1: Understand the Marketplace and Customer Needs and Wants 23
  Step 2: Design a Customer-Driven Marketing Strategy 24
  Step 3: Construct an Integrated Marketing Program That Delivers
  Superior Value 25
  Step 4: Build Profitable Relationships and Create Customer Delight 27
  Step 5: Capture Value from Customers to Create Profits and Customer
  Equity 28
Summary 29
References 30

Chapter Overview

Most of you are already marketing experts. You make marketing decisions and perform marketing activities every day. But while you engage in marketing daily, you may not fully grasp the concept of marketing or know how to practice good marketing for business success. Some have said that "successful companies have one thing in common, they are strongly customer focused and heavily committed to marketing. These companies share a passion for understanding and satisfying customer needs in well-defined target markets" (Kotler & Armstrong, 2012, p. 4). In this chapter, we will look at exactly what marketing is and how it applies to organization development (OD) consultants and service-oriented businesses. We will also provide OD consultants with the marketing tools to acquire and build relationships with customers for the long run and ultimately create successful businesses.

This chapter will lay the groundwork for subsequent chapters by providing a list of definitions of key marketing terms (see Table 2.1), an

Table 2.1 Definitions of Key Terms

- Competitive advantage—an advantage over competitors gained by offering greater customer value, either by having lower prices or providing more benefits to justify higher prices
- Customer satisfaction—the extent to which a product's perceived performance matches a buyer's expectations
- Customer-perceived value—the customer's evaluation of the difference between all the benefits and all the costs of a marketing offer relative to those of competing offers
- Customer relationship management (CRM)—managing detailed customer information about individual customers and carefully managing customer touch points to maximize customer loyalty
- Market segmentation—dividing a market into smaller segments of buyers with distinct needs, characteristics, or behaviors that might require separate marketing strategies or mixes
- Marketing—the process by which companies create value for customers and build strong customer relationships to capture value from customers in return
- Marketing mix—the set of tactical marketing tools—product, price, place, and promotion—that the firm blends to produce the response it wants from the target market
- Positioning—arranging for a market offering to occupy a clear, distinctive, and desirable place relative to competing products in the minds of target consumers
- Target market—a set of buyers sharing common needs or characteristics that the company decides to serve
- Value proposition—the full positioning of a brand—the full mix of benefits on which it is positioned (Kotler & Armstrong, 2012)

overview of marketing, the unique elements of service-oriented businesses and the challenges of marketing OD consulting, and the steps in the marketing process. Ultimately, it will outline an action plan for OD consultants to implement the marketing process and increase business success. While this chapter will provide an overview of marketing for the OD consultant, subsequent chapters will provide more marketing strategies to successfully execute the marketing process relative to their unique value proposition and competitive advantage. This includes strategies for segmenting and targeting the market, communicating with your target market, selling your OD services, and measuring and evaluating the effects of your OD services.

Marketing Overview

Marketing is trying to gain customer attention for your product or service and then convincing people to buy it. Because a consultant is by definition someone who has influence over an individual, group, or organization, customers must first like the person before they will evaluate whether your service has value for them (Block, 2011). For OD consultants, your product is you, the person, and the set of services you have chosen to specialize in and provide for your customers. Those customers that you have created your services for and that you target are your target market. The target market is defined as the set of buyers sharing common needs or characteristics that your company serves or that group of consumers you have identified as those who would be interested in and find value in your services (Kotler & Armstrong, 2012). You need to find the most efficient and effective way to join your targeted customers with your company's services, keeping in mind the price they will pay, the manner in which they expect to receive the services, and the outlets through which they would expect to learn about your services. This, in laypersons' terms, is *marketing*.

Marketing Defined

In the business context, the accepted definition of marketing is the process by which companies create value for customers and build strong customer relationships to capture value from customers in return (Kotler & Armstrong, 2012). As you can see from Figure 2.1, marketing is a cycle

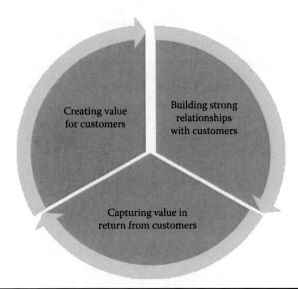

Figure 2.1   Three stages in the marketing process.

with three stages, all of which focus on the customer. All three stages must be present for marketing to occur, completing the full cycle each time you market your services. As you read through the three stages, reflect on how you are fulfilling each of the three stages of marketing in your OD consulting firm. Table 2.2 provides a worksheet for you to determine the three stages of marketing in your firm. As you fill in your answers, keep in mind that each of the three stages of marketing should all center on the customer.

Table 2.2   The Three Stages of Marketing

Directions: Fill in the answers for each of the different stages of marketing in your firm. Business Name: _____ Date: _____		
Marketing Stage	*Question*	*Answer*
Creating value for customers	How will you create value for your clients?	
Building meaningful relationships with customers	How will you build relationships with your clients?	
Capturing value in return from customers	How will you capture value from your customers?	

Creating Value for Customers

The first stage of marketing is creating value for the customer. While it is important in marketing to tell your target market about your service as much as possible, your service must have value for the customer for them to pay attention to your message. So what is value? Value, or customer-perceived value from a marketing perspective, is the customer's evaluation of the difference between all the benefits and all the costs of a marketing offer relative to those of competing offers (Kotler & Armstrong, 2012). Therefore, the onus is on your firm to know your customers, understand what constitutes value to them, and ultimately deliver that value. When the value you deliver to the customer outweighs the cost to the customer, then the customer is satisfied. In marketing, that is called customer satisfaction. However, when the value or benefit to the customer far outweighs the cost to the customer, the customer is experiencing customer delight. That is what all businesses, no matter what the product category, should shoot for.

What is the value of your service? How does your consulting firm deliver value to your clients? You must define your unique skills, competencies, and capabilities to determine your value. Your value might be the ability to build trust in an organization, or your ability to make personal connections with your clients. Whatever your value, you must be able to clearly define it and effectively communicate it to your clients so they perceive your services as valuable.

Building Strong Relationships with Customers

If your marketing message resonates with your target market and they find value in your service, they will be more likely to purchase your service. Once a customer purchases your service, you need to have a plan in place to build a meaningful and lasting relationship with them. It sounds simple, but many companies forget this step and rather focus only on transactions and not on building relationships with their customers for the long-run. Different from transactions, relationships are bonds that give customers a reason to continue doing business with you and help your brand stay top-of-mind. Relationships are what provide companies with a solid customer base. Service-oriented businesses in particular should always try new and improved ways to build deep, meaningful relationships with their customers. It is much easier to keep and grow current customers than to attract new customers. Too much customer engagement is never enough in today's competitive market.

How are you building meaningful relationships with your clients? What are you doing in your consulting firm to keep clients for the long run? You might be making personal connections and building trust, or tailoring your services to meet client needs. Remember, getting clients is only the first step, keeping them and building relationships with them is far more important.

Capturing Value in Return from Customers

The final stage in marketing and the reason you are in business is to make money. Capturing value from the customer means capturing those sales and profits. When the marketing cycle works, your business has figured out how to create a valuable service for your target market, built lasting relationship with them, and captured value or revenues and profits from them in return.

How will you capture value from your clients? In order to capture value from your client, you must determine a price for your OD consulting services. The price or fee that you charge must be equal to the client's perceived value of your service. How you determine your fees depends on what you believe your time is worth in each client situation. You also must be willing to adjust your fees, in some cases upward, to protect the value of your brand. Ultimately, if you don't value your time, the client certainly won't.

Now that you have a better idea of what marketing should accomplish for a business, and how the three-stage marketing cycle works, we need to discuss some of the key differences of marketing a service versus marketing a tangible product.

Marketing Services for the OD Consultant

As an OD consultant, you are marketing your services. Service-oriented businesses face challenges marketing to the customer from a communications standpoint. Four elements are unique to services—intangibility, inconsistency, inseparability, and inventory—referred to as the four I's of services (Kerin, Hartley, & Rudelius, 2013). Each of these elements could become an obstacle for OD consultants and other service-oriented businesses.

Therefore, those in the service sector must identify marketing strategies to overcome each of these special characteristics of services. Each of these four unique service elements is described next in more detail.

Intangibility

Services are intangible, which means you can't see, touch, taste, or examine them before you buy them (Kerin et al., 2013). While a tangible product has characteristics that allow customers to interact with and determine if it is the right product for them, an intangible product, or a service, isn't so easy for a customer to evaluate. And while you can market a tangible product based on characteristics like features, style, and design, an intangible product's characteristics are much harder to define and communicate to the customer. The customer must take the word of the person trying to sell the service that it will work. Customers don't know if the service will work until after the service is performed for them (Hayden, 2013).

So when you buy a service, what are you really buying? While services are intangible, those tangible features of services that firms provide convince customers to buy. Therefore, it is imperative that you provide tangible features, like that of tangible products, to help your customers make good decisions about your service. Tangible features that service firms should promote are as follows.

People. These are every service-oriented business's most important tangible asset. Customers will automatically judge the value of the service by the people who provide it. If they like you, they will be more likely to want to do business with you. Similarly, if they perceive you as a specialist in the field, they will be more apt to want to hire you for their business. If you are an external OD consultant, you need to make yourself and your services known by making contact with potential clients. There are many ways you can get in front of potential clients, including attending conferences, making presentations, writing articles, and engaging in professional networking (Barrow, 2003).

Information. Explain to potential customers how the service will be performed and what the expected results will be. You will also need to have strong, clearly stated guarantees of performance (Berman & Evans, 2013). As an OD consultant, you should create a benefit statement about the services you offer that addresses issues that clients are facing today. This information may be stated in more general terms on your company website and press kits but needs to be conveyed more specifically in customer proposals. Also, be sure to utilize professional networks to tell people what you are doing in your consulting firm (Barrow, 2003).

Customer testimonials. If your clients are satisfied, it means you are doing your job right. Now take the time to ask those happy customers for a few words about how your consulting firm helped their business. Customer testimonials are word-of-mouth marketing that can be very effective for your business (Grieser, 2013). Testimonials "transform your sales pitch into a credible, unbiased recommendation for your product" (Gehl, 2014). Customer testimonials are the most powerful pages on your website because they tell people not only that your service is legitimate but also that other people are seeing great results from it (Hines, 2011). However, it is your job to make sure that only the right testimonials are shown to the public to help promote your business. The answers to the following two questions will help ensure you are collecting and distributing good customer testimonials that will ultimately bring credit to your consulting firm.

Question 1: What makes a good testimonial?

- *Key benefits.* A good testimonial is filled with the key benefits of using your service.
- *Credibility.* To be a good testimonial, you need to establish credibility. This is as easy as including the first and last name and hometown of the testimonial giver and a photo.
- *Comparative.* Testimonials should contain something comparative about your service, like what didn't work for the customer before they tried your service (Gehl, 2014).

Question 2: How should you collect the customer testimonials?

- Link on your website.
- Create an autoresponder that contacts your buyers after they've purchased your product to ask how they're enjoying the product.
- Ask for permission from happy customers to use their letters or e-mails on your website.
- Offer free services to start collecting customer testimonials if you have done little business (Gehl, 2014).

Written proof of your services. Your webpage, brochures, and business cards all provide written proof about what your consulting business provides. Potential customers can read about your company from both you and your satisfied customers and make judgments about whether your particular services are right for them.

- ■ Your webpage should include items like your capability statement, customer testimonials, and a customer account section for current customers to access their account information.

Inconsistency

Because services depend on the people who provide them, their quality varies with each person's capabilities and day-to-day job performance (Kerin et al., 2013). You can decrease inconsistency of the delivery of your service through regular training and observations of your employees. This will ensure that all of your consultants are providing the same quality services at the same quality level. Providing this consistency among your workforce will help alleviate the burden of the owner being exclusively requested to perform all services for the firm. Developing and implementing systematic procedures for performing each service will also decrease the variability of the service each time it is requested. Computerizing your services, no matter how small the firm, is highly recommended to keep services consistent among customers (Berman & Evans, 2013).

Inseparability

Another problem with marketing services is inseparability, or the difficulty of the consumer to separate the deliverer of the service from the service itself (Kerin et al., 2013). The more physical interaction that takes place between the service provider and the customer, the more inseparability becomes a problem for the consumer. Again, proper training of all consultants and standardization of the delivery of the services will help promote your firm's brand rather than its individual consultants. Also, bringing in multiple consultants or rotating consultants on each job will promote customer reliance on your brand rather than the individual consultants. This will help ensure that customers won't leave if a popular employee goes to another firm (Berman & Evans, 2013).

For a successful OD effort to occur, you must develop the internal resources within the organization to limit their dependency on you. Managerial training and educational programs are ways to build leader competence in the firm, leading to the ability to sustain a change effort long after you separate from the firm (Boss, 1983).

Inventory

Services, unlike tangible products, cannot be inventoried. Instead, if the OD consultant gets no appointment to perform his/her service, that time slot or day is lost forever (Kerin et al., 2013). Therefore, you need to carefully plan each work day to optimize service visits or calls. In addition, be prepared to work longer hours during peak periods and perform alternative tasks during slower times (Berman & Evans, 2013). You should also continually build a client pool throughout the life of your business. This consists of people and organizations that you want to work with and plan to pursue actively as clients (Hayden, 2013). There are many sources for client leads. The primary source is referral building. Make sure you are asking for referrals from all of your satisfied clients. Utilize and stay in contact with all of your networks, both personal and professional, and capitalize on that constant communication. Other sources to build your client pool include presenting at those same events where you network. For example, rather than simply attending a trade or professional association meeting or conference, plan to be a speaker (Hayden, 2013). This will enhance your credibility with the group. Another great source for building your pool of clients is writing. For example, a well-written article on a subject of interest to your target market will not only get their attention but also demonstrate your expertise in the field (Hayden, 2013).

Now that you have an overview of the function of marketing from a service-oriented standpoint and you understand the special characteristics of services, you need to know how to put marketing into action in your business. Marketers call this a marketing program. Your marketing program comprises pinpointing your firm's target market and designing an integrated marketing program to deliver value to them. You can do this by following the steps in the marketing process outlined next.

The Marketing Process

The marketing process is a five-step process that will provide you with the steps to follow and build a marketing program for your consulting firm. The five steps of the marketing process are the following:

1. Understand the marketplace and customer needs and wants
2. Design a customer-driven marketing strategy
3. Construct an integrated marketing program that delivers superior value
4. Build profitable relationships and create customer delight
5. Capture value from customers to create profits and customer equity (Armstrong & Kotler, 2015).

Creating value for the customer and building customer relationships is covered in the first four steps, while capturing value from the customer in return is covered in the last step. As we go through each step, we will provide goals and action plans for you to make each step more attainable for your OD consulting firm.

Step 1: Understand the Marketplace and Customer Needs and Wants

Goal 1. Find out what your competition is doing.

Action plan. It is easier than ever today with technology to research your competition in the marketplace. Search your competition on the web, analyze competitor websites to determine what others in your field are doing, or ask potential clients what consulting services they are paying for, from which companies, and why. There are many ways you can bolster your understanding of the marketplace and your competition. The key is to continue to research. The more you know about your industry, the better your chance of staying ahead of the competition.

Goal 2. Determine the needs and wants of your target consumer. Find out which customers are looking for your services.

Action Plan. This requires more research to uncover exactly what services your potential customers are looking for from your business. You can survey potential clients by e-mail, phone, or regular mail. Another option is to provide a link to a survey on your website for those potential clients looking for more information. You may also want to conduct interviews with potential clients face-to-face to uncover more possible services you hadn't thought of.

Once you have determined the needs of your target customer, you must figure out the wants. A potential client might recognize a need for a succession plan at his/her organization. Their want then becomes how they fulfill that need. Do they want to create the succession plan themselves within the organization? Are they looking to hire a consultant to research their company and create one for them? Do they want to hire you, an OD consultant, to work with the company to help them prepare and implement their own succession plan? There is no right or wrong answer, only poor marketing that failed to put your OD consulting firm in the minds of the consumers who had a problem in their organization without a clear solution. They may have needed someone to help them create an open, problem-solving climate throughout their organization (Boss, 1983) but never thought of you.

Ultimately, this first step of the marketing process is staying ahead of both the marketplace and the consumer. For potential clients to want to purchase your services, they need to know that your business can meet their needs and wants. Therefore, you need to continually research to know what services are in demand so that when customers are looking for that service, they call you and not the competition.

Step 2: Design a Customer-Driven Marketing Strategy

You first select which customers to do business with based on segmenting the market. Then you decide on a value proposition by differentiating and positioning your service to your target market so they will perceive value and purchase your service.

Goal 1. To determine what types of clients you can best serve and where they exist, you need to segment the market. There are many ways you can segment the market. Examples of segmentation may include multiple demographic variables and be based on the location, size, or culture of the company. Based on what you determined about the market for your product and your potential customer, you will need to pick a segment or multiple segments and define your target market. Again, your target market is the set of buyers who share common needs or characteristics that your company serves. Your target market is who you will target all of your marketing activities toward.

Action Plan. When firms have a well-defined target market, communicating with potential clients and getting them to want to buy your service becomes a little bit easier. If you have defined your target market as established businesses of over 50 employees and/or $1 million in annual sales, you have a clearer picture of who you are talking to. You need to continue to research businesses that fall into this category so you understand how they think, what they are looking for from OD consultants, and how and why they buy. Ultimately, you want to know what will make them purchase your services or think to purchase your services before that of the competition. From this point forward, all of your marketing actions will be centered on that customer group or target market. Everything from choosing a price for your services affordable for that group, to deciding how you will promote your services (i.e., website, public speaking engagements, etc.) to that group, emanates from the research you uncover about the segment and their buying behavior.

Goal 2. Next, you will need to differentiate your market offering to create superior customer value.

Action Plan. Consulting is a crowded market. So how do you make your OD consulting services stand out in a crowded market? You make them special to your target market, that is, create value in that service for the market you targeted. In marketing, we call this your competitive advantage. So what is your competitive advantage? What is that thing you do better than other OD consultants? Maybe it is the OD interventions that your firm specializes in (i.e., talent management). Maybe your consultants have more experience than most consulting firms. Maybe your company has worked with many companies with proven success. Maybe your prices are lower than the competition or you have a money-back guarantee. Whatever your competitive advantage, it has to (1) be perceived as a valuable benefit by your target market and (2) be something that your target market will pay for.

Goal 3. You need to position your market offering in the minds of the target customer.

Action Plan. Once you have defined your competitive advantage or what you do best as an OD consultant, you need to position your service among others in your same product category. Positioning is the firm's strategy to create a certain image about your product based on your competitive advantage. Therefore, if you choose to be the low-price leader of OD consulting services, the position you want to occupy relative to other OD consultants is to be the lowest price. So when businesses are looking for OD services but are working with a small budget, your firm should come to mind first. When you have created an image for your service that is understood by customers, positioning has been achieved.

Step 3: Construct an Integrated Marketing Program That Delivers Superior Value

Goal. Now that you have defined your target market and your unique selling proposition, you will need to develop a marketing program to reach that customer group and communicate the value of your service.

Action Plan. You can build this program through your marketing mix or 4 P's. The 4 P's of the marketing mix are the product, price, place, and promotion that the firm blends to produce the response it wants from the target market (Kerin et al., 2013). For an OD consultant, the product is your services, price is what you charge for your services, place is the channel or channels you use to distribute your services to your customers, and promotion is how you communicate with potential customers about your services. Now that your target market is defined, you will need to build your marketing mix around them. All of the planning of your marketing mix must focus on the target customer, your competitive advantage, and your chosen position. Table 2.3 shows an example of how a marketing program for an OD consulting firm might look.

Table 2.4 provides a worksheet for you to determine the elements of the marketing program for your firm. As you fill in your answers, keep in mind that each element of your marketing mix (4 P's) should be consistent with the other elements and with the target market you will serve.

Table 2.3 Sample Marketing Program for XYZ Consulting Firm

Element	*XYZ Consulting Firm's Marketing Program*
Target market	Established businesses of more than 50 employees and/or $1 million in annual sales
Competitive advantage	We provide quality service with proven expertise as OD consultants
Positioning	We offer a premium level of service and expect to receive premium compensation for those services
Product	We provide a variety of valuable services that enable a business to run successfully, specializing in change management, talent management, and team development
Price	We offer a premium product at a premium price that provides the greatest value to our customers
Place	We distribute our services at the customer's place of operation
Promotion	We communicate our services to our target market through a multitiered marketing campaign. This includes • Direct sales • Networking • Customer referrals • Website with a page devoted to customer testimonials • Business cards and brochures

Table 2.4   Simple Marketing Program Worksheet for OD Consultants

Directions: Fill in each Marketing Program Element for your firm. Business Name: _____ Date: _____	
Element	*Your Marketing Program*
Target Market	
Competitive Advantage	
Positioning	
Product	
Price	
Place	
Promotion	

Step 4: Build Profitable Relationships and Create Customer Delight

Goal. Now that you have clients, you need to figure out how to keep them for the long run. It is easier for businesses to keep current customers than to get new ones.

Action Plan. How do you keep your current clients? You need to build meaningful, long-term relationships with them. This is accomplished through delivering a product that lives up to its promise and creating customer satisfaction. If you promise your OD consulting firm will provide a variety of valuable services that will enable a business to run successfully, you need to deliver that to the customer. If customers who have purchased and used your services are satisfied, you need to nurture that customer so they continue to do business with you. Some simple ways to keep your customers coming back are to stay in contact with them and always ask for referrals. Staying in contact is as easy as a phone call, an e-mail, or even a personal visit.

If a customer is not satisfied with the quality of your service, you need to follow up with them too. And while they might not become long-term customers, it is important that your firm knows which customers are dissatisfied and why. Service firms can easily put systems in place to provide dissatisfied customers a forum to complain. This could be as simple as administering a survey for customers to fill out after implementing your service. If customers are dissatisfied, you will need to contact them and make it right. This will not only increase the chance of repeat business with that customer but also lessen the chance of them spreading negative word-of-mouth about your business.

Another way to analyze performance is the balanced scorecard. This measurement tool can track company strategy and help facilitate organizational improvement or change (Andrews, 2012). For the OD consultant, it can help you stay focused on the job at hand and detect trouble in the organization before it is too late.

Step 5: Capture Value from Customers to Create Profits and Customer Equity

Goal. Now that you have followed the first four steps of the marketing process and created value for your clients, you need to proceed to the fifth and final step and capture value from them in the form of sales and profits.

Action Plan. Capturing value from customers relies on good customer management. While all customers are important, some may be more profitable for the company than others. If you know enough about your customers, you can manage your relationships with them more effectively for business success. An easy way to better understand and manage your customers is through a classification tool that measures customer relationship groups based on their profitability and loyalty. Each relationship group is managed differently based on its level of profitability and loyalty. The four relationship groups and the recommended management strategies are presented in Table 2.5.

The steps of the marketing process outlined in this section are used as a guide for your business's marketing plan. While each of the steps must be present for marketing to work, your particular firm may focus more on certain steps than on others. Similarly, your firm may have other strategies in your action plan you feel work best for you. If not, use the action plans presented here as a guide that can be manipulated to meet your firm's specific needs.

Table 2.5   Customer Relationship Groups

Customer Group	Characteristics	Management Strategy
Strangers	Low potential profitability and little projected loyalty.	Companies shouldn't invest in this customer group at all.
Butterflies	Potentially profitable but not loyal. There is a good fit between the company's offering and their needs, but like a real butterfly, this customer is not interested in loyalty to one company and will eventually fly away.	Companies should invest time in this group, capturing as much business as they can while they are buying.
True friends	Both profitable and loyal. There is a strong fit between their needs and the company's offerings.	Companies should continue to invest in this group, building long-term relationships with them.
Barnacles	Highly loyal but not very profitable. There is a limited fit between their needs and the company's offerings. Like barnacles on a ship, they create drag or are problematic customers.	Companies should discontinue doing business with this group unless they can improve their profitability (Armstrong & Kotler, 2015).

Summary

The purpose of this chapter was to provide the reader with an overview of the fundamentals of marketing. In this chapter, we covered the characteristics of service-oriented firms, the five steps in the marketing process, and some actionable steps that OD consultants can put into practice immediately to market their firms to their target consumers. The ultimate goal of this chapter was to provide a link between applying the marketing concepts and the OD consultants' increased probability of business success. While this chapter provided the overview, subsequent chapters will provide more action plans for each aspect of marketing your business. After reading this chapter, OD consultants should be better equipped to achieve their business goals.

References

Andrews, M. (2012). 6 tools every business consultant should know. Retrieved from http://www.dce.harvard.edu/professional/blog/6-tools-every-business-consultant-should-know

Armstrong, G., & Kotler, P. (2015). *Marketing an introduction* (12th ed.). Upper Saddle River, NJ: Pearson Education.

Barrow, K. (2003). Marketing your consulting services. *Organization Development Journal, 21*(1), 91–93. Retrieved from https://brainmass.com/file/1535801/pro+quest++t-test+study.rtf

Berman, B., & Evans, J. (2013). *Retail management. A strategic approach* (12th ed.). Upper Saddle River, NJ: Pearson Education.

Block, P. (2011). *Flawless consulting* (3rd ed.). San Francisco, CA: Pfeiffer.

Boss, R. W. (1983). How to select an OD consultant. *Public Administration Quarterly, 7*(1), 115–127. doi:http://dx.doi.org/10.1108/17506200710779521

Gehl, D. (2014). How to effectively use testimonials. Retrieved March 7, 2015, from www.entrepreneur.com/article/83752

Grieser, S. (2013). 12 posts to perfect your customer testimonials. Retrieved March 7, 2015, from unbounce.com/online-marketing/perfect-your-customer-testimonials

Hayden, C. J. (2013). *Get clients now! A 28-day marketing program for professionals, consultants, and coaches* (3rd ed.). New York: Amacom.

Hines, K. (2011). 7 creative ways to get customer testimonials. Retrieved March 7, 2015, from https://blog.kissmetrics.com/customer-testimonials

Kerin, R., Hartley, S., & Rudelius, W. (2013). *Marketing* (11th ed.). New York: McGraw Hill Irwin.

Kotler, P., & Armstrong, G. (2012). *Principles of marketing* (14th ed.). Upper Saddle River, NJ: Pearson Education.

Chapter 3

Evaluating Personal Strengths and Weaknesses: A Competency-Based Approach

Jong Gyu Park

Contents

Competencies for OD Consultants 32
Consulting Styles of OD Consultants 34
Prepare Capability Statement...46
Summary 49
References 49

Organization development (OD) consultants have specific goals for generating more revenue from their most important clients and hottest prospects. If they are to reach these goals, above all, OD consultants must know themselves and clearly understand their strengths and weaknesses as an OD consultant.

This chapter, "Evaluating Personal Strengths and Weaknesses: A Competency-Based Approach," is being used successfully by OD consultants to collect and synthesize objective information about competencies—knowledge, skills, and abilities you have. The competencies help you establish a guideline to self-diagnosis about yourself, allowing you to concisely convey a sincere attempt to better understand your own strengths and weaknesses. The chapter provides a one-page display of the strengths and weaknesses you gain through OD consulting competencies list.

In addition to OD competencies, a successful OD consultant should be aware of his or her personal consulting style. He or she must be able to flexibly change his or her inherent consulting style to perform a variety of roles to accommodate the needs of the client in diverse situations. This chapter will help you identify your personal style in consulting and help you understand various consulting styles so that you can become a more flexible OD consultant.

A capability statement is an important marketing tool used to attract clients. To create an effective capability statement, you first need to identify your strengths and opportunities as an OD consultant. Equipped with this knowledge, you can create a more powerful and consistent message in the capability statement. The last part of this chapter introduces the components and tips for writing a capability statement that will lead you to prepare a more powerful capability statement as an OD consultant.

Competencies for OD Consultants

What is needed to become a successful OD consultant? How can an OD consultant achieve good consulting performance? In order to answer these questions, in this section, we will look at OD competencies that create a successful OD.

Let us look at the definition of a competency. Spencer and Spencer (1993, p. 9) defined the term this way, "an underlying characteristic of an individual that is causally related to…superior performance in a job or situation." David Dubois (1998) has suggested that competency is "those characteristics-knowledge, skills, mindsets, thought patterns, and the like when used whether singularly or in combinations, result in successful performance'" (p. v). According to Rothwell (2012), competencies is a characteristic of a successful performer since it leads to successful work results. Thus, the concept of OD competencies may be defined as desirable behaviors based on a combination of knowledge and skills that create competitive advantage as an OD consultant.

OD is about participative change efforts. While change can be achieved through several means—coercion and persuasion are among common ones selected—the goal of the OD consultants is to harness the creative power of a group and help the group direct its creativity to addressing the problem.

For OD consultants, they never try to substitute their wisdom for the client's wisdom. As a consequence, OD consultants function in a way quite different from the management consultant, who brings expert problem solving and knowledge of the subject area of the problem to a situation.

Thus, OD consultants need appropriate competencies to perform their job in an effective way. OD competency can be defined as "any 'personal quality' that contributes to the successful practice of OD" (Rothwell, Stavros, & Sullivan, 2010, p. 6). What specific quality should OD professionals possess?

Throughout the history of OD, many OD scholars and practitioners have studied about specialized knowledge or skills or competencies needed to perform OD consultation successfully (e.g., Church, Wadowski, & Burke, 1996; Eubanks, Marshall, & O'Driscoll, 1990; Worley & Feyerherm, 2003; Worley, Rothwell, & Sullivan, 2010). This chapter will introduce two study results on OD competencies that can give practical help.

The Organization Development Network is an international, professional association that was established by OD professionals aiming for theoretical and practical development of the OD field. Various information and training opportunity related to OD can be accessed by visiting its homepage (http://www.odnetwork.org). OD competencies suggested by the OD Network (see http://www.odnetwork.org/?page=ODCompetencies) were prepared by Roland L. Sullivan, William J. Rothwell, and Chris G. Worley in 2001. These competencies lists are created based on data collected from more than 3,000 OD practitioners of the OD Network, OD institutes, and Minnesota OD Networks. A total of 141 organization change and development competencies from these lists are classified under 17 subdomains according to OD process: marketing, enrolling, contracting, mini-assessment, data gathering, diagnosis, feedback, planning, participation, intervention, evaluation, follow-up, adoption, separation, self-awareness, interpersonal, and others (for reference, OD Network is currently—November 2015—conducting a survey with not only OD network members but also OD professionals in order to develop global OD competencies).

Worley et al. (2010) conducted a survey with 364 OD professionals, who worked for private organizations in the United States and held master's degrees, in order to refine and develop previously mentioned 141 OD competencies lists (Cady & Shoup, 2015). In the survey, the essential competencies for OD practitioners were asked. The survey revealed the importance of the 23 competencies, such as self-mastery, ability to evaluate change, clarify data needs, manage transition and institutionalization, integrate theory and practice, stay current in technology, ability to work with large systems, participatively create a good implementation plan, understand research methods, manage diversity, clarify roles, address power, keep an open mind, manage client ownership of change, be comfortable with ambiguity, manage the separation, see the whole picture, set the conditions for positive change, focus on relevance and flexibility, use data to adjust for change, be available to multiple stakeholders, build realistic relationships, good client choice, and clarify outcomes.

The OD competencies mentioned previously include the vast knowledge and skills and a variety of abilities and attitudes that an OD professional should have. An OD consultant should identify his or her own strengths and weaknesses by studying these various OD competencies, as this will be the prerequisite to effectively market his or her OD consultancy services (Table 3.1). The worksheet in Table 3.1 will help you assess yourself as an OD consultant. The worksheet was designed to evaluate your current state based on the OD consulting competencies and to identify areas you need to develop. More specifically, because general OD competencies can be found in the works of Worley et al. (2010), the self-assessment in this chapter focused on the OD consulting competencies needed by OD consultants working as external consultants to effectively market your business.

Consulting Styles of OD Consultants

In addition to the OD competencies discussed earlier, you need to be aware of your own consulting style in order to identify your strengths and weaknesses as an OD consultant. Needless to say, it is ideal to be an effective OD consultant to your client. However, when providing support to your client, it is very important to intervene in a useful manner only up to the extent that your client needs help. Therefore, an effective OD consultant should be flexible. He or she should be able to adapt to the client's changing needs and draw out their participation. In other words, he or she must adhere to the underlying values and philosophy of OD consulting. Even if the client demands a clear solution from the consultant, he or she must not violate the underlying philosophy of OD consulting by giving direct directions, proposing solutions, or using persuasion as in the style of management consulting (Marshak, 2014). If possible, the consultant must deliver consulting services in a way that can maximize client participation and he or she must at the same time flexibly apply the level of participation according to the client's

Table 3.1   A Worksheet for OD Consultants' Competency Self-Assessment

Directions: Use this self-assessment to identify your strengths and weaknesses as an OD consultant. It is to be used for you to get an idea of the development needs you face as a successful OD consultant. Give yourself a rating based on your own impressions about yourself. Use the following scale for the right column: 1 = No need; 2 = Some need; 3 = Need; 4 = Much need; 5 = Very great need.

| Areas | Competencies | Representative Behaviors | How Much Need for Professional Development? | | | | |
			No Need	*Some Need*	*Need*	*Much Need*	*Very Great Need*
Technical skill	Analyzing and solving problems	Proactively prompt clients to recognize the potential impact on their business of current and future opportunities	1	2	3	4	5
		Effectively analyze and consider the impact of technical decisions on potential profit, return on investment, and other financial measures	1	2	3	4	5
		Respond to client inquiries about complex technical issues in a way that maximizes understanding	1	2	3	4	5
	Improving work methods	Identify areas of possible process improvement involving the work of other stakeholders	1	2	3	4	5

(Continued)

Table 3.1 (Continued)   A Worksheet for OD Consultants' Competency Self-Assessment

Directions: Use this self-assessment to identify your strengths and weaknesses as an OD consultant. It is to be used for you to get an idea of the development needs you face as a successful OD consultant. Give yourself a rating based on your own impressions about yourself. Use the following scale for the right column: 1 = No need; 2 = Some need; 3 = Need; 4 = Much need; 5 = Very great need.

Areas	Competencies	Representative Behaviors	How Much Need for Professional Development?				
			No Need	Some Need	Need	Much Need	Very Great Need
		Consider the use of technology to improve business processes	1	2	3	4	5
		Monitor budget and revenue expenditures against operational effectiveness	1	2	3	4	5
Client skill	Managing client relationships	Establish good relationships with clients and prospects in order to fully understand their wants and needs	1	2	3	4	5
		Develop, maintain, and facilitate strong relationships with senior-level clients and prospects, even during difficult interactions	1	2	3	4	5
		Consult regularly on large, complex, often multidisciplinary projects	1	2	3	4	5

(Continued)

Table 3.1 (Continued)   A Worksheet for OD Consultants' Competency Self-Assessment

Directions: Use this self-assessment to identify your strengths and weaknesses as an OD consultant. It is to be used for you to get an idea of the development needs you face as a successful OD consultant. Give yourself a rating based on your own impressions about yourself. Use the following scale for the right column: 1 = No need; 2 = Some need; 3 = Need; 4 = Much need; 5 = Very great need.

Areas	Competencies	Representative Behaviors	How Much Need for Professional Development?				
			No Need	*Some Need*	*Need*	*Much Need*	*Very Great Need*
	Generating profitable new business opportunities	Use marketing strategies to develop business within and across area of responsibility	1	2	3	4	5
		Ensure potential new business opportunities are actively pursued to conclusion	1	2	3	4	5
		Keep abreast with the marketplace and apply knowledge to develop new business	1	2	3	4	5
	Strategically managing client satisfaction	Identify and remove barriers in the implementation of better ways of providing client service	1	2	3	4	5
		Proactively seek ways of improving service to clients	1	2	3	4	5

(Continued)

Table 3.1 (Continued) A Worksheet for OD Consultants' Competency Self-Assessment

Directions: Use this self-assessment to identify your strengths and weaknesses as an OD consultant. It is to be used for you to get an idea of the development needs you face as a successful OD consultant. Give yourself a rating based on your own impressions about yourself. Use the following scale for the right column: 1 = No need; 2 = Some need; 3 = Need; 4 = Much need; 5 = Very great need.

Areas	Competencies	Representative Behaviors	How Much Need for Professional Development?				
			No Need	*Some Need*	*Need*	*Much Need*	*Very Great Need*
		Evaluate regularly the effectiveness of service improvements	1	2	3	4	5
Managing skill	Managing and communicating information	Use information to forecast trends and variation in performance against plans	1	2	3	4	5
		Use communication skills to negotiate complex matters where there are conflicting sources of information or opinions	1	2	3	4	5
		Communicate financial performance to inform and motivate associates	1	2	3	4	5

(Continued)

Table 3.1 (Continued)   A Worksheet for OD Consultants' Competency Self-Assessment

Directions: Use this self-assessment to identify your strengths and weaknesses as an OD consultant. It is to be used for you to get an idea of the development needs you face as a successful OD consultant. Give yourself a rating based on your own impressions about yourself. Use the following scale for the right column: 1 = No need; 2 = Some need; 3 = Need; 4 = Much need; 5 = Very great need.

Areas	Competencies	Representative Behaviors	How Much Need for Professional Development?				
			No Need	Some Need	Need	Much Need	Very Great Need
	Working in and leading teams	Create cost and resource project plans while controlling, monitoring, and coordinating activities within the project team	1	2	3	4	5
		Manage communications within project team and to the client	1	2	3	4	5
		Deliver projects on time and within budget	1	2	3	4	5
	Developing yourself and the team's performance	Accurately evaluate the competence and development needs of self and team members against established standards	1	2	3	4	5
		Manage team members effectively, providing opportunities for development through the allocation of work experiences	1	2	3	4	5
		Develop self and coach/mentor others	1	2	3	4	5

situation and consulting circumstances. Simply put, he or she must readily be able to change his or her consulting style.

Consultants are individuals with unique personal styles. However, if the unique consulting style is firmly fixed and restrains flexible action, then this will limit the effectiveness of consulting. Therefore, it is important to know one's own personal style and other consulting types that can be applied to different situations.

Gordon Lippitt and Ronald Lippitt (1986), in *The Consulting Process in Action*, developed eight role models that can be seen as a general consulting type. The eight roles reflect the different levels of intervention by the consultant in a project, in other words, the level of influence that the consultant has on the client. In Table 3.2, consultant roles toward the top are less instructive and there is greater client participation, while consultant roles toward the bottom tend to intervene and participate more directly. For example, the "objective observer" on top is the least directive, which means that decision making is usually done by the client. Opposite of this is the "advocate" on the very bottom, where the consultant takes on the decision-making role and therefore is more directive towards the client.

An OD consultant needs to take on various consulting styles and play the role according to that style. Sometimes, he or she might need to become a "process consultant," while on other occasions, he or she might need to become a "joint problem solver." If the client requests, the consultant might have to play the role of "trainer." However, as an "information specialist" and "advocate," the consultant becomes too instructive, and the client becomes overly dependent on the consultant, so it is not an ideal style for an OD consultant. OD consultants are different from management consultants and need to refrain from being instructive if possible.

You, as an OD consultant, will want to identify your current consulting style and play the role of a stable yet flexible OD consultant. Answer the following questions to reflect on the strengths and weaknesses you have as an OD consultant.

- What is your personal consulting style? Are you client centered or consultant centered?
- Does your current consulting style work as a strength or weakness as an OD consultant? Why?
- How flexible are you as an OD consultant? Can you easily switch to another style if your client or situation calls for it?

Table 3.2 Different Roles and Responsibilities of Consultants

Titles	Roles and Responsibilities of Consultants	Consulting Style		Locus for Decision Making	
		Nondirective	Directive	Client Centered	Consultant Centered
Objective observer	• Poses questions that induces the client to reflect on the problem and solution • Does not directly introduce the consultant's thoughts or ideas • Observes the client's behavior and provides feedback • Asks effective questions that will make the client confront the problem clearly, and supports the client's decision making	●	○	●	○
Process consultant	• Observes the client's problem-solving process and provides feedback • Observes people and conducts interviews to diagnose the client's process and issues • Identifies the dynamics between people or groups that affect the problem solving process • Reports objective data to the client to improve the relationship dynamics and process	●	○	●	◕

(Continued)

Table 3.2 (Continued)   Different Roles and Responsibilities of Consultants

Titles	Roles and Responsibilities of Consultants	Consulting Style		Locus for Decision Making	
		Nondirective	*Directive*	*Client Centered*	*Consultant Centered*
Fact finder	• Plays the role of researcher by gathering facts and stimulating the client's thoughts • Gathers and verifies various information and facts through interviews, surveys, observation, document analysis, etc. • Gathers and interprets core area information that is of importance to the client • Through this process, evaluates whether the process the client has in place is effective or not	◑	◔	◕	◔
Identifier of alternatives and linker to resources	• Checks the alternative solutions and materials and provides outcome evaluation • Checks the alternative solutions for the issue and sets up a standard to evaluate each solution • Predicts the overall outcome of each alternative and provides related material that will help the client solve the problem • Does not directly intervene in the final selection of solution	◑	◑	◕	◑

(Continued)

Table 3.2 (Continued)   Different Roles and Responsibilities of Consultants

Titles	Roles and Responsibilities of Consultants	Consulting Style		Locus for Decision Making	
		Nondirective	Directive	Client Centered	Consultant Centered
Joint problem solver	• Provides alternative solutions and participates in the decision making • Studies the client and problem and actively works to solve the problem (plays an important role in the client's decision making) • Develops solution options with the client and evaluates them and selects the solution • Plays the role of arbitrator as a third party when there is a conflict in the problem solving process	◒	◓	◒	◓
Trainer	• Trains and develops the client • Provides lectures, information, or various training opportunities to the client • As a trainer, the consultant identifies the training needs and sets training goals, designs the training experience and program, and plays the role of group facilitator	◔	◐	◒	◔

(Continued)

Table 3.2 (Continued) Different Roles and Responsibilities of Consultants

Titles	Roles and Responsibilities of Consultants	Consulting Style		Locus for Decision Making	
		Nondirective	Directive	Client Centered	Consultant Centered
Information specialist	• As a content expert, defines whether the approach to the problem is correct • The client has the responsibility to define the issue first, then the consultant plays a directive role to the client until the client adjusts to the recommended approach • The client may become more dependent on the consultant with time. When the client becomes highly dependent on the consultant, they are less likely to consider different alternatives, and are at risk of settling for a weak solution	○	●	◔	●

(Continued)

Table 3.2 (Continued) Different Roles and Responsibilities of Consultants

Titles	Roles and Responsibilities of Consultants	Consulting Style		Locus for Decision Making	
		Nondirective	*Directive*	*Client Centered*	*Consultant Centered*
Advocate	• Proposes, persuades, and instructs in the problem solving process • The consultant intentionally drives the client to take the ideal direction • The consultant yields power and influence so that his/her idea and values are reflected in the problem solving process or solution • As an advocate of a solution, the consultant tries to influence the purpose and method selected by the client • As an advocate of a process, the consultant tries to influence the methodology that is at the base of the client's problem solving behavior	○	●	○	●

Note: ● Very high, ◕ high, ◔ medium, ◑ low, ○ very low.

- Is there a consulting role you do not take often? How could you incorporate this role more to support your client?
- If you have a directive style, how could you become nondirective and more client centered?

Prepare Capability Statement

A capability statement is a document you prepare to promote yourself as an OD consultant or to market your services. It introduces you (or your organization); promotes your capabilities, skills, and competencies; shows your competitive edge over your competitors; and explains why the client should hire you as an OD consultant. In other words, a capability statement highlights the strengths that you or your organization have as an OD consultant or OD consulting firm and serves as the first step that will persuade the potential client to purchase your services.

The capability statement is important because for one, it is included as part of the proposal. The proposal is a core factor needed to win the bidding war. In particular, preparing a better capability statement and proposal than your competitors are a core competency that will decide you and your company's fate in the fiercely competitive OD consulting market. Therefore, do not hurry to prepare your capability statement after your client requests for it, but prepare in advance by identifying your strengths and weaknesses, emphasizing your strength, and mitigating your weakness in advance to prepare a robust capability statement.

There are different types of capability statements, but generally, a capability statement will include the following basic information of yourself and your organization:

- Brief background about your organization's goals and history
- Types of consulting services you can offer
- Subjects in which you can train
- Methodology used, i.e. case studies, group work, panel discussions, interactive activities, etc.
- Your ability to help participants design an action plan to be implemented upon their return
- Demonstration of your expertise in particular regions of the world
- Possible business or industry sectors in which you can coordinate internships

- Information on other services you provide
- Location of previous work or where you have the capacity to conduct either domestic or international work
- Examples of your experience in working with others
- Name of the primary contact at your organization for requests

Here, I briefly explain how to write out five factors among various factors that must be included in your capability statement.

Organization overview. This is the introduction of the capability statement where you briefly describe the business background. It will include where and when you started your business and what is your area of expertise in consulting, etc. It is very important to show that you as an individual or your company is continuously growing. If you are preparing a more detailed capability statement, then you might also include the mission statement or the organization's vision and business philosophy. In case of a short capability statement, organization overview can be often omitted.

Core competencies. This is your unique value proposition to your client that describes your core competencies. Core competencies are the special benefits you can deliver to your client and the source that clearly separates you from your competitors. It includes your unique skills, technology set, etc. Core competencies are a must for a successful performance.

Past performances. Make a list of your past clients and projects. If possible, list projects and sectors relevant to the client that is going to review the capability statement. Including irrelevant past references might actually even backfire. Sometimes, you might include the contact information (e.g., e-mail, mobile phone) of the person-in-charge of the listed past projects. Or you might include previous client's testimonials, endorsements, and positive quotes to increase credibility.

Differentiators. You will describe how you and your company are unique and superior compared to your competitors and why the client should choose your consulting firm above others. Explain what you are going to do to meet the core needs of your client and how it is different from what other competitors can deliver. You might explain about differentiated products or services or human resources, in other words, what differentiating point each consultant has to offer.

Corporate data. This will include the geographical locations of where you are conducting business, the company address, contact number, e-mail address, website, and other contact details. It is a good idea to include the names, positions, and personal contact numbers of the key persons.

If needed, include the company's financial data or firm size. Nowadays, potential clients refer to the consulting firms' websites to check the basic corporate data and various products and services provided by the consulting firm, so it is very important to keep the firm website constantly updated.

Table 3.3 is a simple one-page illustration of a capability statement that briefly introduces your firm to a potential client. Other capability statements could be in different forms depending on their purpose. It could be included in a proposal following an RFP (Request for Proposal), or it could

Table 3.3 Sample Capability Statement

Core Competencies
The core competencies of the organization focus around competency work and seminar design and delivery.
Past Performances
Among previous assignments, ABC, LLC was the lead for the XYZ competency study entitled XYZ Models for Human Performance Improvement (1996) and its update XYZ Models for Human Performance, 2nd ed. (2000), XYZ Models for Workplace Learning and Performance (1999) with XYZ's 2004 competency study Mapping the Future (2004) with D company. Additionally, ABC, LLC was the lead for the 2007–2008 Pulse Check Update of Mapping the Future without D company. Over the years, ABC, LLC has also offered training on a global basis in cooperation with many international partners. Among them are many seminars offered with the Penang, Malaysia-based Institute for Training and Development (offering seminars in the Philippines, Malaysia, Thailand, and Vietnam), Shanghai Jiao tong University in China, Siemens China, Motorola University China, Singapore Institute of Management, Vital Training in South Africa, and Salvo Global (based in Singapore) for sessions in Hong Kong, South Africa, Singapore, and Indonesia. A long list of training sessions offered can be provided on demand.
Differentiators
A major differentiator of ABC, LLC is that it has been involved as primary or subcontractor for all major XYZ competency studies since 1996.
Company Data
ABC, LLC was formally founded in year 2000 but operated under the personal name of OOO (current CEO of ABC, LLC) prior to that date. It is an "s" corporation. Its FEIN is OO-OOOOOOO. The company has 4 full-time employees, but draws on a large number of graduate students with experience from ABC University. ABC, LLC serves a global audience. If you have further questions, please contact Jong Gyu Park (pvj5055@gmail.com, (OOO) OOO-OOOO), senior partner of ABC, LLC.

be a brochure-type, or it could be in the form of a presentation to a client in a meeting to introduce the firm's capability. Recently, many individual OD consultants and OD consulting firms are including their capability statement on their website.

Regardless of what form the capability statement takes, you should not forget that it has to highlight your strengths and deliver your key message in a brief and visually interesting way. While it is acceptable to reuse a well-prepared capability statement, it is also necessary to modify it according to the client's characteristics and the project type. For example, the capability statement for the government sector or nonprofit organization and the capability sector for the profit-sector would have to emphasize different points. You must update your capability statement based on the latest information while maintaining the same context.

Summary

This chapter looked at important presteps in effective OD marketing. You explored the criteria and method of identifying your strengths and weaknesses as an OD consultant. You learned which OD competencies are needed by an OD professional and learned to identify your strengths and the competencies you need to develop from the list. In addition, this chapter discussed the various consulting styles and how one needs to flexibly adapt his or her personal style to the role that the client demands. After objectively evaluating yourself, you should have realized what you need to change or develop to become a more successful OD consultant. Lastly, this chapter looked at what a capability statement is, what components it should include, and some tips on how to develop an effective capability statement. Preparing a powerful capability statement starts with "knowing yourself," as the title of this chapter, "Evaluating Personal Strengths and Weaknesses," implies.

References

Cady, S. H., & Shoup, Z. D. (2015). Competencies for success. In W. J. Rothwell, J. M. Stravros, & R. L. Sullivan. (Eds.). *Practicing organization development: Leading transformation and change* (4th ed., pp. 117–133). San Francisco: Wiley.

Church, A. H., Wadowski, J., & Burke, W. W. (1996). OD practitioners as facilitators of change: An analysis of survey results. *Group & Organization Management*, *21*(1), 22–66.

Dubois, D. D. (1998). *The competency casebook*. Silver Spring, MD: International Society for Performance Improvement.

Eubanks, J. L., Marshall, J. B., & O'Driscoll, M. P. (1990). A competency model for OD practitioners. *Training and Development Journal, 44*(11), 85–90.

Marshak, R. J. (2014). Organization development as an evolving field of practice. In C. G. Worley., A. McCloskey., & M. Brazzel. (Eds.). *The NTL handbook of organization development and change: Principles, practices, and perspectives* (pp. 3–24). San Francisco: Wiley.

Rothwell, W. J. (2012). Career planning and development, and why you should care about it. In W. J. Rothwell. (Executive Ed.), J. Lindholm., K. K. Yarrish., & A. G. Zabellero. (Vol. eds.). *The encyclopedia of human resource management: HR forms and job aids* (pp. 41–47). San Francisco: Pfeiffer.

Rothwell, W. J., Stravros, J. M., & Sullivan, R. L. (2010). Introduction. In W. J. Rothwell, J. M. Stravros, R. L. Sullivan, & A. Sullivan. (Eds.). *Practicing organization development: A guide for leading change* (3rd ed., pp. 1–8). San Francisco: Pfeiffer.

Spencer, L. M., & Spencer, S. M. (1993). *Competence at work: Models for superior performance*. New York: John Wiley & Sons.

Worley, C. G., & Feyerherm, A. E. (2003). Reflections on the future of organization development. *The Journal of Applied Behavioral Science, 39*(1), 97–115.

Worley, C. G., Rothwell, W. J., & Sullivan, R. L. (2010). Competencies of OD practitioners. In W. J. Rothwell, J. M. Stravros, R. L. Sullivan, & A. Sullivan. (Eds.). *Practicing organization development: A guide for leading change* (3rd ed., pp. 107–135). San Francisco: Pfeiffer.

Chapter 4

Evaluating Unmet Needs and Opportunities

Marie Carasco-Saul

Contents

Business Case Study 53
    Creating a Parameter-Based Niche Consulting Practice 53
        Case Discussion 53
Niche Market Identification...54
    Parameter-Based Niche Consulting 55
    Success Factors in Niche Marketing 56
    Pitfalls of Niche Marketing...57
        Tool—Determining Strengths for a Niche Market Consulting Service 58
Personal Branding for Niche Consulting in OD 61
Strategy Development: Strategic Planning for Marketing Consulting
Services 63
    Market Analysis and Evaluation..63
    Value Proposition Development...64
    Entrepreneurial Marketing Strategies...66
    Niche Marketing Strategies..66
    Worksheet—Increasing Your Alternative Customer Base........................67
    Why Marketing Plans Are Overlooked..68
Summary 69
References 69

This chapter will provide an introduction to actionable steps and resources for organization development (OD), change management, and performance management consultants to evaluate unmet needs and opportunities through a niche market for consulting services. The chapter will cover the following areas:

- Niche market identification
- Strategy development: strategic planning for marketing consulting services

According to the Bureau of Labor Statistics, "employment in the management, scientific, and technical consulting services industry is expected to grow by 83 percent (more than 800,000 jobs) over the 2008–18 decade, which is both the fastest projected rate of growth and the largest expected job gain of all detailed industries" (http://www.bls.gov/opub/ted/2011/ted _20110502.htm). Although consulting techniques vary, OD and change management consultants are more closely aligned with the management consulting services per this expected growth trend. With this tremendous growth projection underway, current and future consultants are challenged to stand out from the competition in both service offering and marketing strategy.

The market is saturated with books about consulting but not about marketing OD and performance consulting. This book will fill that gap by providing tools that will aid practitioners in strategically navigating this competitive consulting marketplace. This chapter will provide a foundation on which to help consultants avoid the trap of blind enthusiasm. Through planned market analysis, you will understand where and how your skills could add the most value and how to increase visibility of those skills. Adequate preparation in identifying suitable niche consulting services may also help to increase the credibility of consultants in the broader marketplace by encouraging consulting project alignment with key strengths. This chapter will help answer questions such as the following:

- What is a niche market consulting practice?
- How can a consultant identify a niche to appropriately market services?
- What are the steps to develop a strategic plan for marketing consulting services?

After an introduction to the concepts of niche marketing, including success factors and pitfalls in niche consulting, we will apply these concepts to niche consulting in OD.

Business Case Study

Creating a Parameter-Based Niche Consulting Practice

Dr. John Carter, president of the Gestalt Center for Organization Systems Development (Gestalt OSD), is a highly requested applied behavioral science consultant with over 40 years of experience. When his consulting practice required upward of 70% travel, he sought opportunities in his local town of Cleveland, Ohio, to spend more time with his growing family.

Driven by an interest to have more time at home, Dr. Carter sought corporate work in Cleveland but soon realized that conflicts of interest with previous corporate clients prevented him from working with targeted companies. Understanding that Cleveland had a large healthcare sector, he shifted his focus from corporations to large healthcare institutions, with no prior experience in the sector.

After identifying two organizations, Dr. Carter met with institutional representatives and began the entry phase of the action research model by explaining his interest in working in Cleveland, after which he then argued how his local presence would allow him to offer a lower rate due to travel expenses not being part of the proposed fee. Dr. Carter then established the parameters whereby he could consult. He presented a clear vision on the particular work he wanted to do and the conditions under which he would work. The prospective clients then had the option to consider if those parameters were in line with the organization needs.

Over the next one-and-a-half to two years, the first agency offered him approximately six consulting projects, all of which he turned down since they did not meet his parameters. The second agency offered 10 consulting projects, none of which met his criteria and were also turned down. Interestingly enough, the human resources (HR) lead of the second agency contacted Dr. Carter about a project proposal that would be sent to him and cautioned that he not turn it down. The HR lead explained that although the forthcoming project didn't meet three of his expressed parameters, those items would be addressed within three months. Dr. Carter accepted the project and continued working with the institution for 10 years. See Table 4.1 for definitions of key chapter terminology.

Case Discussion

1. Identify the push factors for finding a niche market.
2. Review the importance of a strategic vision.

Table 4.1 Definitions of Key Terminology

Market analysis—"is sometimes used to describe what is more broadly termed 'market research' and sometimes with an emphasis on analysis." Market research may be defined as "a disciplined investigation aimed at discovering what is going on and what is *changing* in the environment. The object is to discover opportunities and threats; and to assess how some intended action might play itself out" (Burton 2011, p. 818).
Niche market strategy—"an emphasis on a particular need or geographic demographic or product segment" (Teplensky et al. 1993, p. 508).
Strategic planning—"forms the basis for securing prospective business opportunities and generally enables business organizations to pursue specific market performance targets over definite periods of time" (Hill 2012, p. 935).
Value proposition—"attempts to demonstrate quantified benefits to prospective users; benefits they will receive through the implementation of your offering. It considers how much your solution costs to buy, implement, and maintain and then details what the savings or advantages are. Value propositions work best when you're selling business-to-business" (Jolly 2008, p. 270).

3. What benefits might the consultant encounter in expressing niche market parameters? What barriers?
4. What are the pitfalls of taking projects outside the consultant's niche?
5. How was negotiation used in the contracting phase from both the client and consultant perspectives?

Niche Market Identification

Niche marketing is not a new concept. For decades, a myriad of approaches to niche marketing have been used globally in firms of various sizes and in diverse industries. For consulting practitioners, evaluating the benefits and potential pitfalls of such an approach is essential. Kotler (2003) describes five key characteristics of niche markets. Niche marketing is all about narrowing products or services by identifying an unmet need that can be filled based on some area of specialization or differentiation. What often results in niche markets are a small customer base and little competition, both of which allow the potential for growth and profitability. Identifying an area of specialization can either be market led or practitioner led. The former requires research of unmet needs and potentially acquiring skills and experience, while the latter leverages a consultant's current skills and experiences.

This section of the chapter will focus on a practitioner-led approach to niche market identification.

In the consulting world, it is not unusual for a practitioner to be a specialist. These areas of specialization can be a combination of what they do (for example, analytics, mergers and acquisitions, divestiture, strategy, individual interventions, group interventions, C-suite work, or working with boards), how they do it (for example, change management, action research, process consultation, appreciative inquiry [AI], or positive psychology), and where they do it (for example, small businesses, healthcare sector, finance industry, oil and gas, nonprofit sector, or the military). The combinations are numerous and can be even more granular. Specialization is foundational to success in a niche market. Two important aspects of differentiation are, first, identifying patterns for possible alignment between the practitioner's skills and client's needs and, second, demonstrating how the practitioner's approach will help the individual or organization achieve an expressed goal. In successful niche markets, customers will pay a premium for and are willing to build business relationships with service providers that can meet their unique needs. If the consultant cannot distinguish himself or herself, competition can stifle. Therefore, establishing what I refer to as a parameter-based niche consulting practice might be the way forward.

Parameter-Based Niche Consulting

Parameter-based niche consulting requires consultants to have a strong understanding of their competencies, strengths, and development areas. With this clarity, the practitioner can establish his or her service offering around key differentials and evaluate readiness and/or a need for change to help in defining marketing tools. The consulting industry can benefit greatly from practitioners who can leverage a particular area of expertise. For example, the competencies of an OD consultant can add tremendous value to an organization interested in bottom–up, stakeholder-centered/developed solutions. These competencies include conceptual skills, consultation skills, and personal attributes related to understanding culture and cross-cultural dynamics, interventions for improving individual, group, and whole organization effectiveness through coaching, project management, and facilitation skills built on self-discipline, self-awareness, control, and perseverance (Rothwell & Sullivan, 2005). These are valuable attributes to certain consulting projects. Areas of niche OD consulting are discussed at the end of this section.

Some consultants might be very effective in one area and setting and ineffective in another. If consultants take on projects outside their niche-based parameters, hypothetically, there are three possible outcomes. First, they would lose market share of their niche; second, they would need to build skills and credibility in the new area; and third, they may fail in the execution of that new area. From a practical standpoint, taking projects you may not be well suited for restricts your availability for projects you are better suited for when they come up. Understanding and respecting your strengths and limitations are important to both your consultant practice and the broader consulting industry. What might appear to be short-term financial gain could damage your reputation in the long-term and might limit future opportunities for yourself and other consultants in the industry. It takes courage, integrity, and a strong ethical compass to turn down projects outside of an area of expertise. Yet, doing so sends a message that the consultant has a high regard for business ethics, which can be a powerful tool in relationship building and cultivating trust across the industry.

Parameter-based niche marketing is about leveraging a consultant's skills and expertise in what, how, and where they do their work to develop a unique personal brand. "In niche marketing you do not only market your product, you also market your business; reputation is key…a solid reputation in the minds of the customers is essential to be successful as a niche marketer" (Dalgic & Leeuw, 1994, p. 43). At the end of this section is a tool designed to help consultants identify strengths for a niche market consulting practice. This tool is also a useful first step in defining your mission, vision, and values discussed later in this chapter in the section on strategy development.

Success Factors in Niche Marketing

According to Toften and Hammervoll (2013), some success factors include "relationship marketing, developing internal dynamic capabilities and building protective barriers" (p. 281). Managing relationships with suppliers and clients in a way that cultivates strong long-term connections is important. According to Dalgic and Leeuw (1994), relationship marketing must do so. Relationship marketing is rooted in a mutually beneficial exchange and has three elements: "identifying and building a database of current and potential customers, delivering differentiated messages to these people, [and] tracking each relationship to monitor the cost of acquiring the consumer and the lifetime value of his purchases" (p. 43).

SEVEN TIPS FOR EFFECTIVE RELATIONSHIP MARKETING

■ Prioritize your relationship focus on identifying what your customers say they need rather than what you think they need.

■ Survey your current or potential customers and track their expressed preferences.

■ Document key reasons for preferences.

■ Determine what it would cost you to meet expressed preferences (for example, additional training and contracting out service).

■ Highlight your expertise in meeting expressed preferences.

■ Stay connected to potential customers by providing low-cost or no-cost information, resources, or events to keep your business as a "go-to option" in the forefront of their minds. A newsletter is a great starting point.

■ Schedule and commit to making contact periodically based on industry appropriateness, shifting between e-mail, phone, and in-person contact.

Developing internal dynamic capabilities are "strategic capabilities that achieve competitive advantage in dynamic conditions" (Toften & Hammervoll, 2010, p. 739), and "strategic capabilities can be defined as the unique bundle of resources and competencies of a firm needed for it to prosper and survive" (Toften & Hammervoll, 2010, p. 738). Dynamic capabilities are what foundationally separate your consulting practice from others.

Building protective barriers is all about limiting new entrants to your niche market. The consultant does so by "building a close relationship with your customers, patents, copyrights, alliances and relationship marketing. Cover all the bases to deter potential competitors" (Dalgic & Leeuw, 1994, p. 53).

Pitfalls of Niche Marketing

Depending on the business, there are potential pitfalls in taking a niche-based marketing approach that can include the "fear of losing control of distribution channel, diminishing niche demand, attracting large competitors and managing the sustainability of the niche" (Toften & Hammervoll,

2013, p. 277). Beyond this, a subtle yet striking fact is overreliance on data that reveal a gap in the market. When evaluating unmet needs and opportunities, it is important not to assume that a niche in one area will exist in another. There may be a gap in a market but no market in the gap (Raynor, 1992). For instance, a niche in one country with a given demographic may not work in another country with that same demographic. Consider for a moment the menu options at McDonald's. The company has allowed tailored menus to suit local expectations. Franchises in Ireland offer cheese bites; in England, a double espresso; and in Singapore, hot or iced Milo (a cocoa-based beverage). These country-specific niche menu items may not work in the United States, and it would be a mistake to assume they can. In the OD field, if consultants are not careful to objectively gather information and analyze it during the diagnosis phase, it is possible to mistakenly see the problem through the lens of their preferred intervention. If the organization culture is top–down, hierarchical with the locus of power highly concentrated at the top of the organization, an AI approach may prove problematic. The social construction nature of AI seeks information on what works well in the organization and what the organization could be. To be effective, this co-construction process must extend beyond senior leaders in the organization. Therefore, taking a performance consulting or a change management approach might be better suited for this culture.

Another potential pitfall in niche marketing is a failure to differentiate your product or service enough from the competition. "With no differentiation at the product level, consumers quickly see through the slick advertising; the product either cannibalizes existing products or fails" (Raynor, 1992, p. 31). Taking the time to examine the market is imperative to avoiding this pitfall. Shortcuts can damage your reputation. I will cover strategies for differentiation in the next section. Use the tool at the end of this section for help in determining your strengths as a first step in identifying an unmet need.

Tool—Determining Strengths for a Niche Market Consulting Service

Step 1. Answer the questions in the boxes or on a sheet of paper. If using a separate sheet of paper, keep track of the questions with the corresponding letters in the far right corner of each box.

Competencies and Strengths	How to Use Skills	Where to Use Skills	Development Areas
What education and/or training do you have that are helpful to your consulting? 1. 2. 3. A	What is your consulting philosophy (for example, things should be bottom–up or top–down)? 1. 2. 3. D	In what setting are you most comfortable (for example, large company, corporate, nonprofit)? If multiple, rank by preference. 1. 2. 3. G	What development areas have been noted on past performance appraisals? 1. 2. 3. J
What consistent positive feedback have you received about specific consulting or other work you have done? 1. 2. 3. B	Is there an intervention approach that you value or use frequently (for example, action research, performance consulting, appreciative inquiry, management consulting etc.)? If multiple, rank by preference. 1. 2. 3. E	Which sector(s) do you find most appealing (for example, healthcare, finance, education, small business)? If multiple, rank by preference. 1. 2. 3. H	What customer survey-feedback highlight areas of poor execution? 1. 2. 3. K

(Continued)

Competencies and Strengths	How to Use Skills	Where to Use Skills	Development Areas
What type of consulting work do you enjoy most? Or want to do (for example, working with individuals, working with teams, strategy, unions)? If multiple, rank by preference. 1. 2. 3. C	What is your preference for collaboration (for example, working primarily alone, working with a small number of contacts, working with multiple people)? 1. F	What settings make you uncomfortable? And what sectors are you less inclined or are opposed to doing consulting work? 1. 2. 3. I	What skills would you prefer not to use as a consultant? If multiple, rank by preference. 1. 2. 3. L

Step 2. After answering the questions in the box, complete the following sentences by substituting the answers from each box based on the letter in the right corner. See template below for guidance.

Template Guide.

My education, and training in A , make me well suited to work with B + C using E . I am most effective when working F in a G setting. It's my preference to work in the H sector(s). Consulting projects related to K + L particularly in an I setting are not the best fit for me.

My education, and training in _____,
make me well suited to work with _____
using _____. I am most effective when working
_____ in a _____setting. It's my preference to
work in the _____sector(s). Consulting projects
related to _____ particularly in a _____ setting
are not the best fit for me.

Personal Branding for Niche Consulting in OD

Some have said that the single greatest determinant of marketing success is brand strategy. To build a successful niche consulting practice in OD, consultants must have a strong personal brand. This personal brand can be based on several factors, including but not limited to levels of organizational change and corresponding approaches to interventions. In OD, there are person-centered interventions, team building, large systems interventions, whole systems transformations, and interlevel dynamics (Rothwell & Sullivan, 2005). If you completed the tool in the previous section, "Determining Strengths for a Niche Market Consulting Service," you will have a solid foundational understanding on the best fit for your training and interests, which could be paired with common OD interventions. Without information on your strengths and limitations, it is impossible to build a consistent brand. It all boils down to one question, what do you want to be known for?

Interventions	Basic Skills	Advanced Training	Suggestions for Toolbox
Person-Centered (Coaching, Mentoring, Training)	Listening Motivating Group facilitation Conflict management	Advanced degree or certificate in behavioral science Giving feedback	Individual assessments (MBTI, 360-Feedback) Certification
Team Building	Group dynamics Facilitation Conflict management	Process consultation Team development	Individual assessment (Thomas-Kilmann Conflict Mode Instrument)
Large Systems (organization-environment relationship)	Business acumen Critical thinking Research Group facilitation Conflict management	Innovation Process-reengineering Political savvy Working with senior leadership	Cultural assessments (Organizational Culture Inventory) Business performance metrics (Balanced Scorecard)

(Continued)

Interventions	Basic Skills	Advanced Training	Suggestions for Toolbox
Whole Systems Transformation	Big picture thinking Working with groups Facilitation Research Group dynamics	Innovation and entrepreneurship Comfort with repetition per the (PDCA cycle— plan, do, check, act)	Cultural and team assessments

It's not just what you do, but how you do it. The "how" has almost infinite possibilities. Do you want to be known for your attention to detail, facilitation style, or interpersonal skills? These can all be key differentiators. If you're uncertain what this area is or could be, ask for feedback from significant others, clients, or educators who have worked with you. They may have observed strengths you may not know of. Once you have a firm grasp on these strengths, it's important to use them in your marketing materials. It is equally important to obtain client testimonials that reflect these strengths and also share them on your marketing platform. It's also important to mention at this point that you think carefully about the projects you take. Unless you will gain additional training in areas that is not your strengths, resist the temptation to take work outside your niche. Doing so will not allow you to build a reputation around your area of expertise. In the spirit of AI, complete the questions in the tool in Figure 4.1 to further develop your niche OD consulting practice.

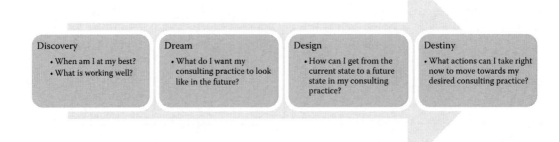

Figure 4.1   Tool—AI 4-D evaluation model for niche OD consulting.

Strategy Development: Strategic Planning for Marketing Consulting Services

Strategic planning is the foundation on which a business evaluates opportunities to pursue over a defined timeframe. It's not just for large organizations. Small businesses and independent consultants can gain tremendous value developing and implementing a strategic plan, especially in marketing services. Although strategic plans vary, most contain a mission statement, vision statement, values, external analysis, internal analysis, competitive advantage, and strategies. For a strategic plan in marketing consulting services, external analysis fits in as part of the market analysis and evaluation, and value proposition development combines the mission, vision, values, internal analysis, and competitive advantage. Developing a strategic plan in marketing consulting services requires an enmeshment of these components with entrepreneurial and niche marketing strategies that lead to action steps for execution. I have developed a framework to be discussed in this section. See Figure 4.2 for a detailed model.

Market Analysis and Evaluation

Another key component used in strategic planning is a market analysis. Research for market analysis can be conducted using surveys, focus groups, archival databases, or telemarketing. The process involves gathering information on trends, competition, and channel of distribution and possible customers that will aid an individual or business in understanding the market

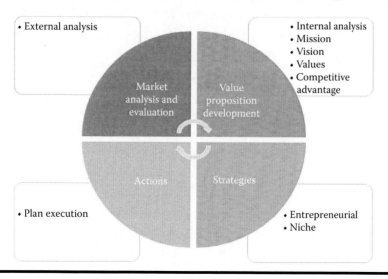

Figure 4.2   Strategic plan for marketing consulting service.

environment. This information is used to develop a marketing plan that out-lines segmentation/niches, segments, customer groups including demographics, and expressed needs. One of the first critical steps in the market analysis is performing an external analysis. The consultant can identify opportunities and potential threats to the development of a marketing plan. Many high visibility projects in the public and private sectors find value in creating advisory groups comprised of key stakeholders. The same approach should be considered by OD consultants. These stakeholders can include customers, suppliers, com-munity leaders, or academics in a local university business school. The goal is to identify influencing forces that shape competition. In his book *Competitive Advantage: Creating and Sustaining Superior Performance*, Porter (1985) outlines five forces shaping competition and profit potential: potential new entrants, bargaining power of buyers, bargaining power of supplier, potential substitute products or services, and rivalry among existing competitors. These areas will be covered in more detail in the context of OD in another chapter.

Value Proposition Development

Having a value proposition is widely regarded as an instrumental part of business strategy. It is the compass that a business uses to direct time and resources and for some is an imperative to consider in strategic planning. Yet, few businesses have one. Many definitions exist for the value proposi-tion concept, but it can be understood as the benefits an organization brings to a client (Hassan, 2012). As part of the strategic plan for marketing consult-ing services, the value proposition stems from a sequence of internal analy-sis, development of a mission, vision, and values, that aid in determining a consultant's competitive advantage.

An internal analysis will reveal your consulting practice strengths and weaknesses by analyzing activities (for example, sales, customer service, supply chain) and financial considerations (for example, cash flow, purchas-ing) in your business (May, 2010). "Vision provides the long-term perspective and your reason for being—*why* you are in business. Mission clarifies your operating focus—*what* you do. Values provide a framework for behavior—*how* you do it" (May, 2010, p. 3). Earlier in this chapter, I discussed inter-nal dynamic capabilities as a competitive advantage because they are the resources and competencies that will allow your consulting practice to stand out from the competition. This is an important aspect of your value proposi-tion. "A value proposition isn't simply a sum showing how many times faster, or cheaper, your offering is. It takes into account how much your solution costs to buy, implement and maintain, and then details what the savings or advantages are. Value propositions work best when you're selling business-to-business" (Jolly, 2008, p. 270).

According to research by Payne and Frow (2014), a value proposition is developed in two stages that involve creating a general industry value statement and a customer-specific value proposition. Foundational to these steps are industry and customer knowledge and partner knowledge. The consultant should identify customer needs from the market analysis and use this understanding to develop a proposition. An illustration of a well-developed value system is detailed by Payne and Frow's assessment of British Telecommunications plc (BT), which had six key proposition areas: "customer relationship management; supply chain management; knowledge management; organizational effectiveness; flexible working; and, e-business" (p. 219). These propositions were based on issues expressed by customers. BT's proposition considered three stakeholder groups: the customer, the organization itself, and suppliers and partners. As a consultant, you must identify key stakeholders to your business. There should also be a focal point (for example, improving quality, customer service, etc.) tied to some measurable financial impact from finish in each initiative.

Jolly (2008) outlines four steps to determine if a new concept will sell or be stagnant:

1. Describe what the prospect could improve: productivity, efficiency, revenues, safety, time to market; what they can reduce: costs, staff turnover; and what they might create: satisfaction, position, new services— by buying from you.
2. Project how much this improvement would be worth in terms of cash and reduced timescales or provide a percentage/range.
3. Talk to your prospective users about what they'll be able to do differently.
4. And get them to agree on what the saving really could be or the extra productivity. Sticking to talking value lets you set the agenda, enables you and the customer to jointly agree on the value, and makes the customer set the price (p. 271).

Ultimately, "there are three elements of the value creation process: determining what value the company provides to its customers; determining what value the company receives from its customers; and, by successfully engaging in this co-creation" (Payne & Frow, 2014, p. 215).

Entrepreneurial Marketing Strategies

Developing a strategy for marketing consulting services requires distinguishing between conventional marketing and entrepreneurial marketing. Kurgun, Bagiran, Ozeren, and Maral (2011) outline 13 areas of distinction. On the entrepreneurial side, in summary, this type of marketing is done by keeping a very close connection to the message that is being shared, primarily via word of mouth. In addition, there is a proactive and deliberate focal point on the customer that influences innovations toward the marketing approach.

Niche Marketing Strategies

Subject matter experts argue that a choice of a niche marketing strategy should occur only under certain conditions. Dalgic and Leeuw (1994) state these conditions are as follows:

- If the company concerned can approach a niche in a manner, better and different than others.
- If the company can create considerable goodwill in a relatively short period, to deter potential competitors.
- To avoid competition/confrontation with larger competitors and to devote its energy to serving a unique market; to enhance an opportunity; survival.
- To use as a competitive strategy to penetrate large markets or existing segments (p. 49).

Other works in the area of niche marketing highlight that niche marketing is a strategy comparable to segmentation that overlaps conceptually for size of markets and firms, number of players, specialization, and using relationship marketing (Toften & Hammervoll, 2013). Dalgic and Leeuw's research (1994) outline 12 critical steps in a niche marketing strategy, summarized as follows:

- Know yourself, your customer, and your competitors
- Develop a database to track client needs
- Distinguish yourself from the competition
- Be careful not to compete with yourself in a particular market
- Build relationships with customers in a way that can stay off competitors

- Don't overdo anything
- Take time to create a strategy
- Pay attention to the market and adjust accordingly
- Think about ways to have an alternative customer base

Worksheet—Increasing Your Alternative Customer Base

Step 1: Identify local businesses that could use your expertise.

- Begin your search with the U.S. Chamber of Commerce directory
  https://www.uschamber.com/chamber/directory
  - This search will help you to identify local Chambers of Commerce chapters in any state.
- Once you have selected a local chapter, navigate to the Business Directory Search.
  - Search for businesses based on alphabetical categories.

Step 2: Develop a list of potential clients based on categories.

- Using an Excel spreadsheet, create individual sheets for various categories of businesses.
- At a minimum, your top row should include a designation for consulting fit, business category name, and the potential client's address, phone number, and key contact person.
  - You can get more granular as you deem appropriate.
- Using the Excel document, filter option for the top row, sort your data based on consulting fit to prioritize the timing of your contact with potential clients.

Template Guide.

Consulting Fit (Choose One)	Category A	Address	Number	Key Contact
Weak Possible Strong	Company Name			

Sample Excel Sheet with One Business Category.

	A	B	C
1	**Consulting Fit**	**Category A: Home & Garden**	**Number**
2	Possible	ABC Carpeting, 777 Lucky Drive, Denver, CO	888-222-1111
3	Strong	MCA Repairs, 678 University Drive, Denver, CO	888-123-4557
4	Strong	Colorado's Own, 888 Oak Lane, Denver, CO	800-OWN-1234
5	Weak	Jolly Maids, 456 Liberty Avenue, Denver, CO	800-555-7777

Step 3: Reach out to a variety of possible clients across multiple categories based on consulting fit.

■ Monitor the responsiveness of businesses in each category to further vet client needs and consulting fit.

"Niche marketing requires a customer/market-oriented organization which is customer focused, competitor oriented, responsive, anticipative and functions in balance with the market and with internal resources; in pursuit of long-term relationships and sustainable profitability" (Dalgic & Leeuw, 1994, p. 53).

Why Marketing Plans Are Overlooked

There are several reasons small-to-medium-sized enterprises (SMEs) have no marketing plan. These reasons include (a) unawareness of the marketing concept, (b) naivety of marketing role, (c) lack of knowledge of the planning process, and (d) marketing's lack of value and limited resources—people, time, money. Among these reasons were three common factors: (1) lack of focus—market orientation, direction, consensus, (2) lack of capability—knowledge, skills, resources, and (3) lack of will—desire, faith, commitment, motivation (Lancaster & Waddelow, 1998). SMEs often have limited time and resources, even more so for an independent consultant. Therefore, having a strategic marketing plan is important to reduce opportunity cost. "Marketing planning often allows the marketing profile to permeate a firm's activities and instills a marketing perspective into activities such as setting objectives, motivating and directing staff, establishing priorities, and improving the quality of market information" (Carson & Cromie, 1989, p. 36). The stages involved in a marketing plan depend on the size and complexity of a business but often include internal and external audits, creating a strategy, then implementing and controlling marketing activities (Carson & Cromie, 1989). Other chapters will discuss value proposition development and market analysis and evaluation in greater detail, including Porter's five forces shaping competition and profit potential.

Summary

This chapter provided an introduction to actionable steps and resources for consultants to evaluate unmet needs and opportunities from the perspective of a niche market for consulting services. The chapter began with a discussion on niche market identification, highlighting both success factors and pitfalls in niche markets. A new concept of parameter-based niche marketing was introduced. The concept defined parameter-based niche marketing as the act of setting consulting boundaries based on a consultant's skills and expertise to develop a unique personal brand. The second section focused on strategic planning for marketing consulting services based on a model built on four key areas: market analysis and evaluation, value proposition development, strategies, and actions. An important distinction was made between conventional marketing and entrepreneurial marketing conditions and the steps required for implementing a niche marketing strategy. The chapter concluded by outlining why marketing plans are overlooked and summarized the important factors to overcome barriers and recapped stages involved in creating a marketing plan.

References

Burton, V. L. (Ed.). (2011). Market research. In *Encyclopedia of small business* (4th ed., Vol. 2, pp. 818–821). Detroit, MI: Gale. Retrieved February 18, 2015, from http://go.galegroup.com/ps/i.do?id=GALE%7CCX2343700360&v=2.1&u=psucic&it=r&p=GVRL&sw=w&asid=6a57ddeb730508d0f7f1a09deecad5f4

Carson, D., & Cromie, S. (1989). Marketing planning in small enterprises: A model and some empirical evidence. *Journal of Marketing Management, 5*(1), 33–49.

Dalgic, T., & Leeuw, M. (1994). Niche marketing revisited: Concept, applications and some European cases. *European Journal of Marketing, 28*(4), 39–55.

Hassan, A. (2012). The value proposition concept in marketing: How customers perceive the value delivered by firms—A study of customer perspectives on supermarkets in Southampton in the United Kingdom. *International Journal of Marketing Studies, 4*(3), 68–87.

Hill, S. D. (Ed.). (2012). Strategic planning. In *Encyclopedia of management* (7th ed., pp. 935–942). Detroit, MI: Gale. Retrieved February 18, 2015, from http://go.galegroup.com/ps/i.do?id=GALE%7CCX4016600283&v=2.1&u=psucic&it=r&p=GVRL&sw=w&asid=bd4ae88a5e725b3d22af67514fd8f89a

Jolly, A. (Ed.). (2008). Create customers before you create products. In *The innovation handbook: How to develop, manage and protect your most profitable ideas* (pp. 270–272). London, England: Kogan. Retrieved February 18, 2015, from http://go.galegroup.com/ps/i.do?id=GALE%7CCX3209400051&v=2.1&u=psucic&it=r&p=GVRL&sw=w&asid=3086931599790a9cce7695426acdecdf

Kotler, P. (2003). *Marketing management.* Upper Saddle River, NJ: Prentice-Hall.

Kurgun, H., Bagiran, D., Ozeren, E., & Maral, B. (2011). Entrepreneurial marketing—The interface between marketing and entrepreneurship: A qualitative research on boutique hotels. *European Journal of Social Sciences, 26*(3), 340–357.

Lancaster, G., & Waddelow, I. (1998). An empirical investigation into the process of strategic marketing planning in SMEs: Its attendant problems, and proposals towards a new practical paradigm. *Journal of Marketing Management, 14,* 853–878.

May, G. L. (2010). *Strategic planning: Fundamentals for small business.* New York: Business Expert Press.

Payne, A., & Frow, P. (2014). Developing superior value propositions: A strategic marketing imperative. *Journal of Service Management, 25*(2), 213–227.

Porter, M. E. (1985). *Competitive advantage: Creating and sustaining superior performance.* New York, London: Free Press.

Raynor, M. E. (1992). The pitfalls of niche marketing. *The Journal of Business Strategy, 13*(2), 29–32.

Rothwell, W. J., & Sullivan, R. L. (Eds.). (2005). *Practicing organization development: A guide for consultants.* San Francisco, CA: John Wiley & Sons.

Teplensky, J. D., Kimberly, J. R., Hillman, A. L., & Schwartz, J. S. (1993). Scope, timing and strategic adjustment in emerging markets: Manufacturer strategies and the case of MRI. *Strategic Management Journal, 14*(7), 505–527. doi:10.1002/smj.4250140703

Toften, K., & Hammervoll, T. (2010). Niche marketing and strategic capabilities: An exploratory study of specialised firms. *Marketing Intelligence & Planning, 28*(6), 736–753.

Toften, K., & Hammervoll, T. (2013). Niche marketing research: Status and challenges. *Marketing Intelligence & Planning, 31*(3), 272–285.

Chapter 5

Proposal Process

Aileen G. Zaballero

Contents

Request for Proposal 72
    Solicited Request..73
        Internal vs. External Solicited Request 74
        Government RFPs 76
        Nongovernment RFPs 76
    Unsolicited Request 76
Target Audience...77
Clarifying Your Role 78
    Contractor 78
    Freelancer...78
    Consultant 78
        OD Consulting 79
        Management Consulting..80
Proposal Writing..80
Financial Terms and Conditions 82
Summary 86
References 89

Writing a compelling proposal is critical to succeed in today's highly competitive business world. Part of the process of marketing is the proposal writing process. This is a consultant's opportunity to pitch why they are the best choice for the job; it is synonymous to an employee's job resume, cover letter, and interview. Writing a proposal is one of the most important processes that a consultant has to learn. First, you must know *who your target audience is*. Each proposal should be written differently based on the specific client's interest. The more knowledgeable you are about the client, the higher the likelihood of getting the contract; this will require research. Next, a consultant must be clear about *what role they will have*. Approaching a proposal as an organization development (OD) consultant will be very different from a proposal as a management consultant. Furthermore, it is important to understand the type of work you will be doing, whether it is a contractor/vendor, a freelancer, or a consultant. What terms you use is more than just semantics; it has legal and contractual considerations. Another important factor in writing a proposal is *what you will be doing*. It will be imperative to have a clear understanding of what the job requires, what the client expects, and what the final deliverables are. It will also be important to know *when the work will be completed*; this will include specific timeline, milestones, and completion dates. Final considerations will be the *where* and *how much*. Where will the project be completed? And, most importantly, how much will it cost?

In this chapter, the author will discuss the basics of the request for proposal (RFP) and key aspects to consider about the client when writing a proposal. Next, the author will further differentiate OD consulting and management consulting and how the proposal reflects the difference, as well as distinguish the difference between work as a contractor/vendor, freelancer, or consultant. Finally, the author will discuss financial considerations. As an additional resource to this chapter, a basic proposal template will be included.

Request for Proposal

Proposals can either be solicited or unsolicited. Many organizations and government agencies will seek out products and services from an outside source; this includes solicitation to solve a specific problem (Turner, 1982). They often will release what is known as an Request for Proposal (RFP). An RFP is a formal document that outlines a problem that needs to be addressed. An RFP is both a document and a process (see Figure 5.1 for illustration). For example, if the Department of Energy (DOE) is seeking opportunities to advance critical education and training to develop the future workforce for the advanced commercial building sector, then the DOE may announce its request in the Commerce Business Daily. "The Commerce Business Daily (CBD) lists notices of proposed government procurement actions, contract awards, sales of government property, and other procurement information.

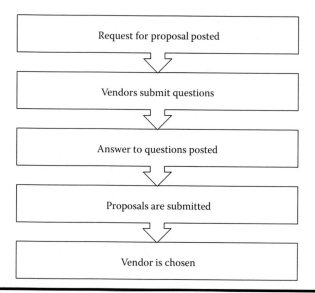

Figure 5.1   RFP process.

Each edition contains approximately 500–1,000 notices" (www.GPO.gov). The proposal is then developed based on the RFP.

Solicited Request

The RFP process generally begins with the request being posted or sent to specific vendor(s). How it is published will depend on where and who is submitting the request. Local, state, and federal government usually have very strict procedures for the RFP process. Vendors will then have a chance to ask for clarifying questions. If the RFP is posted publically, then the response to vendor questions will also be posted publically. It is important to note that the deadlines to submit proposals usually have hard timelines. Once all proposals are reviewed, the vendor is then selected.

The RFP can be sent to

- A specific organization/consultant, referred to as a sole source invitation, where a partnership is being considered (closed RFP);
- A short list of prequalified vendors who have met the qualification requirements (closed RFP);
- A long list of invited vendors who provide the services of product needed (closed RFP); or
- A publically listed announcement (open RFP).

The RFP process is intended to provide structure and transparency to the procurement process and can vary widely. RFPs are an excellent tool for organizations and government to find the best products/services at the best price (Smotrova-Taylor, 2012). In addition, it is an evaluation process for finding the best fit. At a minimum, an RFP should include the following:

■ Relevant background information about the organization submitting the RFP;
■ Explanation of the project scope;
■ Schedule for the work; and
■ Evaluation criteria that includes timeline and any other relevant information.

An RFP typically entails more than a request for cost. Other requested information may include company history, financial information to ensure organizational stability, capability statements, product information, estimated completion time, and consultant references (Sullivan, 2008).

An organization may also send a request for information (RFI) when they are soliciting various vendors with the intent to collect written documents about a vendor's capabilities. RFIs are generally used in the construction industry. A request for tender (RFT) is an open invitation for suppliers and may be legally required to ensure competition and avoid nepotism. A request for quotation (RFQ) invites vendors to the bidding process, also known as the invitation for bid. RFQ is generally used when the client knows what they want but need information on how vendors can meet the specific requirements.

Some requests are very clear and detailed and provide specific information of what should be included in the proposal; others can be more ambiguous. Whether responding to an RFP, RFI, RFT, or RFQ, the consultant must conduct background research in order to compete with other consultants.

Internal vs. External Solicited Request

An understanding of the roles of external and internal consultants is important to consider in solicited RFPs. Traditionally, internal consultants are considered to be members of an organization whose primary job is to assist other people working in other areas of the organization. An internal consultant is someone considered to be an official, often ongoing member of the organization. The relationship of the consultant to the organization is determined usually by a job description and various personnel policies. He or she is paid on the basis of his her ongoing role in the organization (Scott & Barnes, 2011). On the other hand, an external consultant is someone considered not to be an official, ongoing member of the organization. A project's contract is a letter of agreement that determines the relationship between the consultant and the organization. He or she is paid on the basis of a particular project having certain desired results and deliverables.

Many organizations will define the problem and then seek proposals from both internal and external organizations. If the capabilities exist within the organization, most often, the project will stay internal. However, in many cases, the project requires specific skills sets and competencies. Figure 5.2 illustrates the process of a solicited RFP. Some bidding processes will go through multiple rounds to generate the best market price. Government agencies are required to issue RFPs to ensure fair and transparent selection.

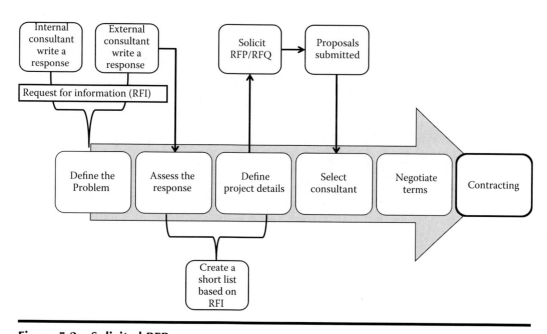

Figure 5.2   Solicited RFP.

Government RFPs

Many businesses fail to take advantage of government contracts and bid opportunities. Many consultants forget that the US federal government is the single largest buyer of goods and services. Knowing how to market to local, state, and federal government agencies can be profitable. However, acquiring contractual work with the government can be tedious and time consuming. An understanding of how they solicit and award contracts is therefore important (Smotrova-Taylor & Springerlink, 2012).

For consultants with very little government contracting experience, this can be an upward battle, so many consulting organizations will hire a professional to help. However, the first step requires identifying where to find the RFPs. Local and state government agencies usually list their RFPs on the purchasing/procurement section on their website. Federal government agencies post their RFPs with the US Government Publishing Office (GPO). "The GPO is responsible for the production and distribution of information products and services for all three branches of the Federal Government" (www .gpo.gov). Federal Digital System (www.fdsys.gov) provides public access to approximately 1200 libraries nationwide and provides advance search capabilities to identify RFPs listed in the Federal Depository. Those who are interested to submit need to be registered as vendors with the government. However, anyone can access the existing list of RFPs. There are several companies whose main service is to list, track, and assist vendors in acquiring RFPs. *FindRFP* concentrates on bidding opportunities with federal, state and local government. The *RFPdatabase* lists both government and nongovernment RFPs.

Nongovernment RFPs

Private or nonprofit organizations do not have the same requirements as the government does. They are not required to publicly post their RFPs to their website. Most often, the organizations will invite "approved vendors." If the proposal is sent to a targeted audience, it is considered a closed RFP, unlike the government RFPs that have to be open. Open RFPs allow any potential contractor to view and submit a bid.

Unsolicited Request

An unsolicited proposal, an organization or consultant will take the initiative and identify a client's problem, write a proposal that addresses the condition so the client is aware of the problem, and then presents a plan of action to solve that problem. Most unsolicited proposals occur internally. For example, a human resource director may write a proposal for the executive team to implement a new enterprise performance management software to transform its current human resource management system.

Target Audience

A proposal will most likely be more relevant if the target audience is considered. This will include knowing the industry, the organization, the department, and, specifically, the client's situation, needs, and desired benefits. If you don't understand the client, you undoubtedly can't propose a solution to resolve their problem. Furthermore, it is possible that what the client states as the problem is not the real problem at all; most often, it is a symptom of the problem. For example, a doctor does not treat a patient's sore throat. A doctor will diagnose the patient's condition and determine if the sore throat is a cold symptom or caused by strep throat. This requires asking the right questions (Freed, Romano & Freed, 2011).

The optimal approach to understanding what the client really needs is to talk with them and to do further research. At a bare minimum, research the organization and its industry. Ask questions about the following:

■ How long has the organization been in business?
■ Who are the key decision makers?
■ What products and/or services do they provide?
■ Who are the major competitors?
■ What is the company's financial situation?

If possible, ask various stakeholders in the organization about their experiences, challenges, and concerns. Review the operating policies and procedures. Examine the organization's management philosophy and culture. Explore if other options have been attempted to address the goals outlined in the RFP and what the outcomes were. Inquire about the organization's previous or current experience with consultants (Freed et al., 2011).

Clarifying Your Role

When writing a proposal, is it important to understand what your role is. A contractor and freelancers are often viewed as temporary workers. A consultant, on the other hand, generally works in an advisory capacity and usually does not do the actual work. In developing the proposal, it will be important how the client uses such terms. It is not uncommon to start off as a consultant and then be pressured into doing work beyond the proposal; this is often referred to *scope creep.* A clear understanding of what the client expects is important, and how you word the proposal will also be equally important (Weiss, 2011).

Contractor

A contractor, for all intents and purposes, is essentially a temporary employee. Most contractors provide a specialized service in return for a fee or compensation. Unlike consultants, contractors actually complete the work. Many organizations use contractors for a particular skill set, such as graphic design or web design, and for a specific period of time. It is important to note that although it may be full-time, it is usually set for a specified amount of time such as a week, number of months, or specific number of years. Most contractors will work with one company at a time and are often expected to maintain office hours.

Freelancer

The terms *contractor* and *freelancer* are frequently interchanged, but they are not synonymous. Most often, a contract employee will work full-/part-time for one client/employer and most likely will work at their site. However, a freelancer usually works from his or her own work/home base and will usually have multiple clients. Freelancers are usually paid by work output and are responsible for their own taxes. Freelancers and most contract workers do not receive employee benefits such as paid vacations, overtime, insurance, 401K, etc.

Consultant

Consults provide advice to clients for remuneration. According to Peter Block (2000), a "consultant is a person in a position to have some influence over an individual, group, or an organization, but who has no direct power to make changes or implement programs" (p. 2). In many organizations, professionals who were once regarded as subject matter experts often transition to a consultant's role. Many consultants work for large consulting firms that offer a wide range of capabilities; other consultants come from academia and assist with problems relating to their specific research or proposed theories. A consultant may also have many roles throughout the project, such as the following:

- Advisor—giving expert advice to solve a problem or achieve a goal.
- Coach—helping individuals clarify and achieve goals and also learn.
- Collaborator/partner—working with people to benefit from the relationship.
- Educator/trainer—helping others develop new knowledge, skills, and insights.
- Expert—providing content expertise in certain areas.
- Facilitator—helping a group to decide what it wants to accomplish and then helping the group to achieve those desired results.
- Problem solver—clarifying problems, using various styles, and approaches to "solve" them.
- Researcher—collecting, organizing, and analyzing information.
- Facilitator—guiding groups or individuals through learning experiences.

Other roles might include analyst, synthesizer, impartial observer, critic, friend, and mentor. These are mostly positive roles. Of course, some people have strong negative impressions of consultants, as well, such as an outsider.

Consultants help businesses identify and implement solutions; how that is done will vary. An advisory consultant will only provide recommendations. Alternatively, an operational and/or functional consultant will provide recommendations and support the implementation process. Process consultants generally focus on the "how to" implement, whereas a technical consultant, focuses on applying his or her specific skill set.

OD Consulting

OD is the practice of helping organizations solve problems and reach their goals. A key emphasis in OD is assisting clients not just in meeting their goal but also with learning new problem-solving skills they can use in the future. OD utilizes what we know about systems, and what we know about human behavior, to plan and manage the development of organizations into thriving, growing, healthy, organic human systems that meet the needs of all their stakeholders. OD practitioners improve the effectiveness of an organization by applying knowledge from the behavior sciences—psychology, sociology, cultural anthropology, and other related disciplines (Schein, 1978; Rothwell et al., 2010).

Management Consulting

Management consulting is generally a contract advisory service provided to organizations in order to identify management problems, analyze them, recommend solutions to these problems, and (when requested) help implement the solutions. Although there are few formal educational or professional requirements to be a consultant, these services are ideally provided by individuals who are specially trained or qualified in a particular field, such as information technology or organizational change, and who strive to provide independent, objective advice to the client organization.

Proposal Writing

"Writing proposals is exhausting work requiring meticulous attention to detail, significant amount of data research, and comprehensive planning" (Barron, 2008, p. 387). The main objective of any proposal is to persuade the potential client that you are the best fit for the job. How you write that proposal will vary and can range from a formal contract to informal letters of agreement. In order to secure the contract, make sure to bid for work that most aligns with your mission, vision, and capabilities.

A sufficient amount of research and planning is needed to prepare an acceptable and feasible proposal. It is recommended to review previously awarded projects, if possible, and identify key factors of a successful proposal. Seek advice from those who have been successful in the proposal process. Many RFPs will include an evaluation rubric. Table 5.1 is an example of an evaluation worksheet.

A good proposal begins with a clear idea of the goals and objectives of the project. Furthermore, the proposal should reference relevant knowledge and current research, specifically citing pertinent current literature. In addition, a good project begins with a sense of why it will be a significant improvement over current practice. Concentrating initially on the goals and objectives helps confirm that the actions are designed to attain those goals.

Table 5.1   Proposal Evaluation Scoring Worksheet

Criteria	Point Value	Grade (10–100%)	Score
Understanding of objectives (10 points)			
• Clearly states the current condition and desired outcomes	5		
• Clearly states the objective of the project	5		
Qualification and experience (15 points)			
• Knowledge and expertise of bidder	5		
• Documented outcomes of bidder's previous projects	5		
• Suitability of proposed staffs' CVs	5		
Proposed methodology/recommendations (25 points)			
• Methodological approach including timetable	5		
• Proposed forms and usefulness of deliverables	5		
• Suitability of proposed data gathering	5		
• Suitability of proposed data analysis/validation	5		
• Suitability of recommendation	5		
Reporting/performance milestones (25 points)			
• Outlines clear deliverables and milestones	5		
• Aligns deliverables with overall project objective	5		
• States specific timelines and completion dates	5		
• Outlines clear deliverables and milestones	5		
• Suitability of proposed data analysis/validation	5		
Accountabilities (10 points)			
• States client's responsibilities	5		
• States consultant's responsibilities	5		
Financial offer (15 points)			
• Overall value for the money	15		
Total	**100**		

After the goals and activities are well defined, deliberate what resources will be necessary, such as people, time, and resources (Weiss, 2011).

Evidence of preliminary work demonstrates planning and commitment to the project and often indicates the project's potential for success. If possible, reference what prework has been completed in preparation for the project. At a minimum, the proposal should include the following (Weiss, 2011):

- *Overview of the situation:* Summarize the current condition and reiterate the desired outcome.
- *Stated objectives:* Clarify the organization's specific objectives.
- *Value:* Explain the value added by meeting the stated objectives and how it aligns with the overall mission of the organization.
- *Metrics:* Designate tangible and measurable indicators of completion. Indicate how the client will evaluate the project.
- *Timing:* State specific timelines and completion dates.
- *Accountabilities:* Clarify the client's responsibilities (i.e., provide documents, access, resources) and reiterate your specific role and responsibilities (i.e., facilitate focus groups, conduct interviews).
- *Capabilities:* Provide credentials and capabilities that indicate why you are the best fit for the job.
- *Financial terms and conditions:* Declare what the financial obligations to complete the work are. Clarify how, when, and under what conditions it should be paid.

Financial Terms and Conditions

The most important consideration in a proposal is the finances. The budget serves as the operational blueprint for spending and outlines the project in fiscal terms. A budget narrative is usually required. This narrative is a one-page statement that justifies budgeted items and allows the client to quickly see if you are within their cost estimate. Depending on the RFP, supporting documents may be included to justify expenses. These expenses should align with the proposal narrative and illustrate how the project will be structured and managed. The budget information will include all activities planned and the personnel who will be required to complete the objectives.

Budget summary is a clear indication of whether a proposed project has been carefully planned and is feasible (Shore & Carfora, 2011).

An accurate assessment of all cost that is deemed as allowable, allocable, reasonable, and necessary will be important to carefully consider. This should include all the costs of any personnel, supplies, and activities required by the project and should be based on actual costs, when possible. Most budgets will include the following (Shore & Carfora, 2011):

- *Direct cost:* Cost that is specifically allocated for the project itself, such as salaries, supplies, travel expenses, phone usage, and printing.
- *Indirect cost:* Cost that cannot be allocated directly to the specific project or program, such as operational, administrative, custodial, and accounting/finance. These costs are often referred to as the "cost of doing business."

Prior to developing the budget, it is recommended to review the narrative and highlight all activities and outline the specific financial implications. Assign each cost to an appropriate budget category. It is suggested to utilize a worksheet, as illustrated in Table 5.2. Cost estimates should be grouped

Table 5.2   Budget Proposal Worksheet

Budget Proposal					
Project Title:					
Duration of Project:		Start Date:		End Date:	
Expenditure Item		*Quantity*	*% of Time*	*Estimated Cost*	*Notes*
Direct Cost					
Personnel					
• Principal Investigator					
• Co-Researcher					
• Research Assistant					
• Other Professionals (i.e., Research Advisor, etc.)					

(Continued)

Table 5.2 (Continued)   Budget Proposal Worksheet

Budget Proposal				
Project Title:				
Duration of Project:	Start Date:		End Date:	
Expenditure Item	*Quantity*	*% of Time*	*Estimated Cost*	*Notes*
• Administrative				
• Tech Support				
• Multi Media Specialist				
Personnel Subtotal				
Equipment/Materials/Supplies				
• Computer Software				
• Computer Hardware				
• Research Publications				
• Documents, i.e., books, articles				
• Phones				
Equipment/Materials Subtotal				
Travel				
• Airfares	# of Trips			
• Per diem ($/day)				
• Car Rental/Taxi	# of Days			
• Hotel	# of Days			
• Phones				
Travel Subtotal				
Publication/Reports				
• Editing and proofreading				
• Translation				
• Cover Design/Graphic Design				
• Layout/Technical Production				

(Continued)

Table 5.2 (Continued)   Budget Proposal Worksheet

Budget Proposal				
Project Title:				
Duration of Project:	Start Date:		End Date:	
Expenditure Item	*Quantity*	*% of Time*	*Estimated Cost*	*Notes*
• Printing				
Publication/Reports Subtotal				
Other Direct Costs				
• Consultant Fees				
• Communication/Internet				
• Other				
Other Direct Cost Subtotal				
Total of Direct Costs				
Indirect Cost				
Overhead or Indirect Cost				
• Accounting Services				
• Auditor and Lawyers Fees				
• Maintenance				
• Office Space				
• Insurance				
• General Project Administration				
• Other				
• Other				
• Other				
Total Indirect Cost				
Grand Total Cost (Total Direct Cost + Total Indirect Cost)				

into subcategories and designated to reflect the critical areas of expense. These expenses should be itemized within the subcategories.

Most RFPs will set the budget guidelines. However, the most important consideration in developing a budget proposal is whether it is realistic. If the budget is too low, it may jeopardize the completion of the project, but if it is too high, you may not be selected for the contract.

Summary

A consulting proposal is an important document and process to master when marketing consulting services. A proposal template (Table 5.3) is provided to guide you. Knowing how to write a clear, effective proposal can help build a consultant's client base. As discussed in this chapter, each proposal should be tailored specifically to the client's needs, interest, and objectives. The more informed you are about the client the higher the likelihood of obtaining the contract for work.

As an OD consultant, the client seeks your specific skill set and capabilities. However, the first access point usually starts with the proposal process that sets the organization on track. This will require careful research and planning. An effective proposal considers the organization's structure and develops a detailed work plan with specific milestones. Measurable deliverables will clarify the expected goals and validate the estimated cost to achieve these goals (Freedman et al., 2001).

Developing an organizational development proposal requires more than a thorough assessment of the RFP. The proposal should also include specific details on how you will conduct a thorough organizational diagnosis to ensure that the identified problem is the real problem. All too often, a proposal is developed based on the perceived problem, therefore providing inappropriate solutions to meet the key objectives (Jones & Brazzel, 2014; Rothwell et al., 2010). To ensure that the objectives are met, identifying the root cause will help ensure that the best solution is proposed.

Table 5.3 Proposal Template

Title of Intervention Proposal
Introduction
The introduction should begin with a compelling statement that encourages the key stakeholder to take action and highlight potential considerations if nothing is done. The current condition and desired outcomes must be clearly stated. Furthermore, the proposal should reference relevant knowledge and current research, specifically citing pertinent current literature, as well as explain the value added by meeting the stated objectives and how it aligns with the overall mission of the organization.
Example:
Skills needed to be successful in today's fast-paced changing environment must be transferrable as jobs and the way work is done continuously changes. The complexity of work is evolving as technology interfaces at multiple levels across all industries. Furthermore, the aging workforce and the rapid growth in new industries continue to create a skills shortage (Darr, 2007 as cited by Hilton, 2008). Therefore, the demand for education and training to produce qualified and competent workers intensifies. These changes necessitate a need to evolve learning interventions from a curriculum-based/hours completed based-program to a competency-based education (CBE).
This section should also include an introduction of the consulting firm.
Example:
Rothwell & Associates, LLC, is an independent consulting firm that focuses on critical issues in human resource development and management. As a full-service consulting firm, we customize all programs to address your specific needs. We will assist your organization to create competency-based education program ...
Objectives
Clarify the client's specific objectives (what did they state as their desired outcome) and the proposed solution (how is the consulting firm going to assist in achieving the outcome)
Overview of the Solution
Lastly, the introduction should include an overview of the proposed solutions. By this point, the reader will determine the following: • Does the consulting firm understand our problem? • Does this consulting firm have the necessary competency to resolve our problem? • Is the solution appropriate for me to read further?

(Continued)

Table 5.3 (Continued)   Proposal Template

Title of Intervention Proposal
Capability Statement
Provide credentials and capabilities that indicate why you are the best fit for the job. The capability statement should include the following: • Core competencies • Differentiators (how are your different from other consulting firms) • Past performance related to the proposal • References related to the proposal • Company data and contact information
Proposed Solution
This section will specify the what, when, where, and how the consulting firm will support the organization.
Recommended Solution
• What will be done (kinds of interventions)? • What resources does the client need? • What resources will the consulting firm provide? • Where will the interventions take place?
Timeline
• When will it begin and end (timeline)?
It is critical that all ambiguities are addressed, including the proposed timeline. If the proposal is accepted, when will the work begin? Remember the negotiation process can take as long as several months. It is suggested that work begins when the contracts are signed and timelines are based on the starting point.
Metrics
• How will completion be measured (how do you know the consulting firm has competed the job)?
Designate tangible and measurable indicators of completion. Indicate how the client will evaluate the project.
Accountabilities
The client's responsibilities must be clearly stated (i.e., provide documents, access, resources) and reiterate your specific role and responsibilities (i.e., facilitate focus groups, conduct interviews).

(Continued)

Table 5.3 (Continued)   Proposal Template

Title of Intervention Proposal
Financial Terms and Conditions
This is the second most important section of the proposal. If the reader reads past the introduction, he or she will most likely go straight to the cost and consider the following question: Can we afford this? Is this within our budget? Is this consulting firm worth this amount?
This narrative is a one-page statement that justifies budgeted items and allows the client to quickly see if you are within their cost estimate. These expenses should align with the proposal narrative and illustrate how the project will be structured and managed.

References

Barron, J. (2008). Top ten secrets to writing award-winning training proposals. *Industrial and Commercial Training, 40*(7), 387–389. doi:10.1108/001978 50810912261

Block, P. (2000). *Flawless consulting: A guide to getting your expertise used* (2nd ed.). San Francisco: Jossey-Bass/Pfeiffer.

Freed, R. C., Romano, J. D., & Freed, S. (2011). *Writing winning business proposals* (3rd ed.). New York: McGraw-Hill.

Freedman, A. M., Zackrison, R. E., & NetLibrary, I. (2001). *Finding your way in the consulting jungle: A guidebook for organization development practitioners.* San Francisco: Jossey-Bass/Pfeiffer.

Hilton, M. (2008). Workshop: Exploring the intersection of science education and the development of 21st century skills. Unpublished document. Division of Behavioral and Social Sciences and Education. Center for Education. Washington, D.C.: The National Academies.

Jones, B. B., & Brazzel, M. (2014). *The NTL handbook of organization development and change: Principles, practices, and perspectives* (2nd ed.). San Francisco: Wiley.

Rothwell, W. J., Stravros, J. M., & Sullivan, R. L. (2010). Introduction. In W. J. Rothwell., J. M. Stravros., R. L. Sullivan., & A. Sullivan. (Eds.). *Practicing organization development: A guide for leading change* (3rd ed., pp. 1–8). San Francisco: Pfeiffer.

Schein, E. H. (1978). The role of the consultant: Content expert or process facilitator? *The Personnel and Guidance Journal, 56*(6), 339.

Scott, B. & Barnes, B.K. (2011). *Consulting on the Inside.* Alexandria, VA: ASTD Press.

Shore, A. & Carfora, J. M. (2011). *The art of funding and implementing ideas: A guide to proposal development and project management.* Thousand Oaks, CA: Sage.

Smotrova-Taylor, O., & SpringerLink (Online service). (2012). *How to get government contracts: Have a slice of the $1 trillion pie* (1st ed.). Berkeley, CA: Apress.

Sullivan, E. A. (2008). Request for proposal. *Marketing News, 42*(3), 8.

Turner, A. N. (1982). *Consulting is more than giving advice.* Boston: Harvard University Graduate School of Business Administration.

Weiss, A. (2011). *The consulting bible: Everything you need to know to create and expand a seven-figure consulting practice.* Hoboken, NJ: Wiley.

Chapter 6

Pricing OD Consulting Services

William J. Rothwell

Contents

Common Pricing Situations...92
How Pricing OD Consulting Differs from Pricing Other Consulting.............95
Philosophical Issues to Consider in Pricing OD Consulting........................96
    Targeted Rate 96
    Market-Based Rate...97
    Consultant-Based Rate..97
    Client-Based Rate..98
    Work-Based Rate 98
    Place-Based Rate..98
    Consistency-Based Rate..99
    Value-Based Rate 99
    Combination 99
    Creative Approaches to Rates 100
Summary...100
Chapter Tool: Pricing OD Consulting Worksheet.......................................101
References 101

Pricing consulting services is a traditional challenge for all consultants, and it poses special challenges for organization development (OD) consultants. Pricing is one of those classic "Ps" in the four or seven Ps of marketing. Others within the classic 4 Ps of marketing include promotion, product, and place, and additional others in the expanded list of 7 Ps of marketing include people, processes, and physical evidence (Goi, 2009).

This chapter examines pricing consulting services in OD. It examines such issues as the following: (1) What are common pricing situations in consulting? (2) What makes the pricing of OD consulting services different from pricing in management or performance consulting? And (3) what philosophical issues should be addressed by OD consultants as they consider their pricing strategies for their work and for their clients?

Common Pricing Situations

Take out a sheet of paper and write down how you would handle each of these pricing situations you may confront. (The author of this chapter has encountered all of these situations.) If you can answer all of them, then you may have a good pricing strategy; if you cannot answer all of them, then you may wish to consider reading the chapter for some guidance on how to handle these, and comparable, situations that may arise in your OD consulting practice.

Situation 1
  You receive an e-mail from someone you do not know and from
    an organization you have never heard of. The e-mail is succinct.
    Between the salutation and the signature, the e-mail simply reads:
    "How much do you charge for consulting?"
Situation 2
  Your OD consulting firm was recently founded. You are having dif-
    ficulty getting business. A promising client comes along from a
    famous organization. As you prepare a budget for the proposal to
    the client, you consider giving the client a reduced rate on the first
    contract so that your firm will have an edge against other consulting
    firms that may compete for the contract.
Situation 3
  You are approached by a nonprofit organization involved with humani-
    tarian efforts. The client asks you for a "discount." The reason the
    client gives you is that the organization is not a profit-making entity.

Situation 4

The human resources (HR) department of a large organization's subsidiary approaches your OD consulting firm for help. This HR department is in a low-wage country in Africa. When you present your proposal, the client asks you to reduce your rate because "this is not the United States, and our subsidiary simply cannot afford to pay US consulting rates."

Situation 5

The internal consultants of an OD department of a large organization ask your OD consulting firm for help. The client indicates that the only work they want to request can be done at your desk and involves reviewing assessment and feedback strategies to be carried out by the internal OD consulting department. Your firm has been asked to serve as "external consultants to coach and advise the internal consultants." You are unsure what to charge for that service that involves no onsite work and involves simply work that could be done at your desk.

Situation 6

A famous international consulting company asks your firm to work on a monthly retainer. The company's leaders offer to sign a contract with your firm after you sign a nondisclosure agreement. In return for pledging some available hours per month, the consulting company will pay your firm a standard rate. If your consulting hours exceed the retainer amount, the consulting company will pay you a prorated amount per hour. If the hours requested in a month do not match what the company has paid for, they will roll over into subsequent months.

Situation 7

You and your OD consulting firm members are approached by consulting firm XXX, located offshore. XXX would like to strike up an arrangement in which their firm can translate and sell tools developed by your consulting firm. XXX would also like a license to operate as an agent for your firm in another nation where English is not widely spoken.

Situation 8

Your OD consulting firm would like to pursue work with different governmental entities. You know that many governmental entities must typically contract with the lowest-price vendor, and you also know that extra points are awarded to vendors as proposals are evaluated when the business is minority owned, woman owned, or veteran owned. Members of your firm suggest appointing a black female veteran as chief executive officer of your business, even though the individual selected for this role is not knowledgeable about OD or about the business.

Situation 9

You are the director of an internal OD consulting department that functions within the HR department of your organization. An operating manager from one of your organization's largest departments approaches you to do a teambuilding project. You write a proposal to the client in a memorandum of agreement (MOA) that stipulates the statement of the problem to be solved and steps in a work plan. The MOA also spells out the work plan, timeline, budget, and staffing mix. After reviewing the MOA, the operating manager asks you to supply a forecast of the return on investment (ROI) that will result from the teambuilding effort.

Situation 10

The HR vice president of a famous multinational company asks you and your OD consulting firm for a proposal for an OD effort. A few weeks later, you receive a polite letter by mail that indicates that the project has been awarded to a different OD consulting firm that was "more in keeping with the organization's business needs." Shortly thereafter, you receive a phone call from a consultant in a different OD consulting firm. The person calling you indicates that his firm has been awarded the contract but has been told to follow your firm's work plan for their estimated hours and budget. The person calling you also indicates that the reason for the call is that he does not understand all elements of your work plan, and he is asking if you will go over it with him at no charge.

Summary of the Situations

Were you able to answer all situations posed? What improvements may be needed to your OD consulting firm's pricing strategies based on your answers to these questions? Write down areas for improvement in how your OD consulting firm manages pricing for services.

How Pricing OD Consulting Differs from Pricing Other Consulting

Pricing OD consulting services differs from pricing other consulting services in management consulting or in performance consulting. There is one major reason why.

Some management consultants take the client's diagnosis of the problem at face value (Kubr, 2002). They do not worry that the client may have misdiagnosed the problem(s) or the solutions needed to address the problem(s). OD consultants cannot afford to do that because clients sometimes confuse symptoms with root causes and sometimes want to throw the wrong interventions at their problems (Zackrison & Freedman, 2003).

In OD, get the diagnosis right first. That means it is often necessary to pose tough questions to the clients about how they know that they have diagnosed the problem properly and have chosen the most effective solution(s) to the problem(s). OD consultants are painfully aware that operating managers, even those professionally trained with MBA degrees, rarely know how to diagnose problems in human systems, how to separate symptoms from root causes, and how to select the most effective solutions to the problems once identified. OD consultants must often persuade the client of the need to diagnose organizational problems first and facilitate a process in which as many key stakeholders as possible agree on problems, agree on solutions, agree on action plans, and agree on the metrics by which to measure success (Worley, Rothwell, & Sullivan, 2010). The latter steps may be a change intervention in its own right and may have to precede action-oriented strategies to address "presenting problems" (symptoms).

Consider a simple example. Managers call in an OD consultant to help reduce turnover in the organization. The problem is defined as "excessive turnover." But OD consultants know that "excessive turnover" is not a root cause but is merely a symptom of some other problem and some other root cause(s). It is essential to find out what those root causes are before proposing a change effort. The challenge is that many clients are unwilling to pay for such a diagnosis from various stakeholders due to cost sensitivity, the belief that management already knows root causes, and that taking time to diagnose issues may lengthen the time to the impact of solutions.

Often, OD consultants may have to propose two separate proposals with two separate pricing structures. One change project is to assess, feed back, and agree on problems and solutions and action plans to implement the solutions. Another change project is to execute the action plan for improvement once identified.

Philosophical Issues to Consider in Pricing OD Consulting

Many philosophical issues emerge as OD consultants carry out their helping strategies with clients (Weisbord, 1981). Consider the following: Should OD consultants base their pricing strategies for consulting rates on a targeted rate, a market-based rate, consultant-based rate, a client-based rate, a work-based rate, a place-based rate, a consistency-based rate, a value-based rate, some combination of these, or some other (and creative) approach? While there are no hard and fast rules that answer all these questions consistently, OD consultants must work out their own answers to these different approaches. What follows is a brief description of each pricing approach.

Targeted Rate

Some clients assume that all consultants have a targeted rate they always apply. It may be based on an hourly rate, a daily rate, or a fixed rate for a project.

Suppose, as an OD consultant, you believe you can make $300,000 per year plus benefits if you were working full-time. Based on that estimated rate, then you should charge for consulting services accordingly. If you earned $300,000 per year (a number picked out of the air for illustrative purposes only), then your benefits might be worth about 50% of that.

That makes your total annual earnings about $450,000 per year. At that rate, your hourly rate (computed by multiplying 22 work days per month by 12 months per year and by 8 hours per day and then dividing that number into $450,000) equals an hourly rate of $213.08 and a daily rate of $1,491.57. It does not stop there. About 50% of a consultant's time should be spent in marketing and about 50% in billable hours. By that logic, you should be charging double the amount listed above for billable hours—which means $426.16 per hour and $3,409.28 per day.

It is possible to do fix-rate work by project. Some clients insist on it. Doing that can make sense to some when the OD consultant has much experience doing a specific kind of change intervention and has time reporting results that provide accurate time estimates for how long it may take a consultant to work with a client to formulate and implement that change.

But fixed-rate projects are usually a bad deal for consultants. One reason is that clients have often misdiagnosed their problems, which necessitates backtracking in the middle of a project to address genuine issues. A second reason is that many variables determine a fixed-rate price, and the OD consultant may not have clear answers to all questions at a project's outset. A third reason is that some clients may insist on additional steps in a project, which can (in turn) lead to "scope creep" that costs the OD consultant who has not anticipated this common consulting problem.

Market-Based Rate

Another way to determine pricing strategy for OD consulting work is to base rates on what "comparable individuals" or "comparable firms" charge (Willmot, 2014). If OD consultants have colleagues who have about the same education, experience, and level of fame in the field who are charging a rate, then perhaps other OD consultants in the same league would be well-advised to benchmark with their colleagues to find out what they charge. Then adjustments can be made.

The problem is that other consultants simply may not tell you the truth about their rates. And they are incented not to do so. After all, if I lie to you and tell you I am charging $30,000 per day and then you follow suit, I am likely to steal your business if I charge a lower rate. While lying is unethical, it happens. The best evidence in benchmarking is based on actual consulting bills from clients, which may be tough to get.

Consultant-Based Rate

Larger OD consulting firms may have a hierarchy of consultants. There may be entry level, supervisory level, and partner level. (Other labels are possible.) But what the client should pay may be based on the estimated or actual hours worked by different levels of consultants. It may be necessary to price a change project based on how many estimated hours are expected for each level of consultant and then add them up.

Client-Based Rate

Some OD consulting firms may charge different rates to different clients. There may be a rate for businesses, nonprofits, and religiously affiliated organizations and governmental entities. And it can become more granular-ized with rates broken out by big, medium, and small organizations.

Work-Based Rate

Does the work require travel or not? Should you charge the same hourly, daily, or project rate for work that requires no travel and work that requires almost continuous travel?

Some OD consultants charge by the work that the client wants. If the client simply wants reviews of materials or preparation of documents, then one rate may be justifiable. But if the client wants onsite work, another rate may apply. Some OD consultants charge more if they have to supervise subcon-tractors, offer executive coaching, or prepare and conduct training as part of a change effort.

Place-Based Rate

Does an OD consultant have one rate applicable globally, or does an OD consultant base rates on the living costs and gross domestic product in other locales? Do you charge the same rate in equatorial Africa you would charge in the Midwestern United States, or that you would charge in New York City or Washington, DC?

There are no hard and fast rules to answer these questions. It is clear, however, that some retailers vary their prices by region and others do not. Walk into a fast-food place in China. You will find they charge the same rate in local currency charged in the United States or in Western Europe. But fast-food is usually a low-cost item, and that is why it can be different for consulting, which may turn into a long-term endeavor.

But one important difference emerges in working abroad: tax issues. Other nations may have higher tax rates than your home country, and some clients may be willing or unwilling to deduct or pay the local taxes for the consul-tant's work. You must meet your tax burden to remain ethical and legal, and the cost of taxes in one place may be significantly higher or lower than in others. That consideration should be part of your global pricing strategy.

Consistency-Based Rate

Consistency is important. If you charge one client a specific rate for an OD change effort, it may be necessary to charge other, comparable organizations the same rate. Remember: clients talk to each other, and they may know what your firm charged another, comparable organization for the same service. While adjustments can be made to reflect annual inflation rates, it is not wise to charge one client a rate and then propose to charge a different organization of the same kind double that rate in the same year.

Value-Based Rate

Some clients insist on ROI or impact-based estimates before, during, or after OD projects (Willmot, 2014). To carry out ROI studies, it is necessary to place a "cost" on a problem (and all of its components) and then place a "benefit" on solving the problem. ROI studies focus on financial issues only. But it is also possible to estimate the "business impact" of an OD intervention by estimating the impact of the change effort on all elements of the organization's strategic balanced scorecard. The balanced scorecard looks at financial, customer, business process, and learning and growth issues affecting an organization, and it is possible to estimate before, during, or after an OD intervention how the change effort affects each quadrant in the scorecard.

Combination

OD consultants may combine any or all approaches listed previously in determining pricing strategies.

But clients will often ask how OD consultants calculated the estimated project cost (and benefits). While transparency is a good thing, and it can make sense to share with clients how costs (and benefits) were determined, care should be taken in doing that. It is typical practice to give a client a ballpark estimate for a change project rather than a spreadsheet breakdown with all assumptions specified. While the consultant should use a spreadsheet to estimate labor costs (on the one hand) and travel, per diem, lodging, and other costs (on the other hand), it is often wise to provide clients with bottom-line estimates of project costs only. To do otherwise is to invite nitpicking that can be detrimental to project planning.

Creative Approaches to Rates

Much experimentation exists in pricing OD change projects.

One issue, often open to negotiation, is ownership of intellectual property rights that arise from materials or approaches developed with one client in cooperation with an OD consultant. It can be negotiated in contracts. If clients worry about project costs, one issue open to negotiation is to provide the client with a discount if intellectual property rights are jointly owned.

Another issue open to negotiation is use of data collected during a project. Some OD consultants work on advanced degrees, and they may be under obligation to publish or perish for their jobs or for pursuing degrees. OD consultants can negotiate a discount for their services if they are given rights to analyze data collected in a project and, with the client's permission, publish them with the organization's name disguised or given for real.

Summary

This chapter focused on the pricing P of the famous marketing questions of product, promotion, and place. The chapter addressed three important questions: (1) What are common pricing situations in consulting? (2) What makes the pricing of OD consulting services different from pricing in management or performance consulting? And (3) what philosophical issues should be addressed by OD consultants as they consider their pricing strategies for their work and for their clients?

The chapter opened with 10 pricing situations, and you were invited to consider whether you or your OD consulting practice could successfully answer all of them. The chapter also noted that OD consulting differs from such other types of consulting as management or performance consulting in that, in OD, the problem is not always known at the outset of the change effort. It may simply be tougher to price a facilitated effort than one in which the consultant plays expert and offers prescriptions to be filled. Finally, the chapter reviewed various philosophies about pricing OD consulting, and these included targeted rates, market-based rates, consultant-based rates, client-based rates, work-based rates, place-based rates, consistency-based rates, value-based rates, some combination of these, or some other (and creative) approaches.

Chapter Tool: Pricing OD Consulting Worksheet

Directions: Use this worksheet to help you think through what you should charge for various OD consulting services. The goal of the worksheet is to decide on hourly and daily rates and to provide caveats for different client projects or work. For each question appearing in the left column, provide your answers in the right column. It may be necessary for you to develop a spreadsheet to ensure consistency across answers and to price specific projects.

	Questions How much does your OD consulting firm wish to be guided by...	Your Answers
1	A targeted rate?	
2	A market-based rate?	
3	A consultant-based rate?	
4	A client-based rate?	
5	A work-based rate?	
6	A place-based rate?	
7	A consistency-based rate?	
8	A value-based rate?	
9	A combination of any or all of the above approaches?	
10	A creative approach to pricing and consulting rates?	

References

Goi, C. L. (2009). A review of marketing mix: 4Ps or more? *International Journal of Marketing Studies, 1*(1), 2–15.

Kubr, M. (2002). *Management consulting: A guide to the profession* (4th ed.). Geneva: International Labour Organization.

Weisbord, M. R. (1981). Some reflections on OD's identity crisis. *Group & Organization Management, 6*(2), 161–175.

Willmot, R. (2014). *Professional services marketing wisdom: How to attract, influence and acquire customers even if you hate selling*. Milton, Australia: John Wiley & Sons.

Worley, C. G., Rothwell, W. J., & Sullivan, R. L. (2010). Competencies of OD practitioners. In W. J. Rothwell., J. M. Stravros., R. L. Sullivan., & A. Sullivan. (Eds.). *Practicing organization development: A guide for leading change* (3rd ed., pp. 107–135). San Francisco: Pfeiffer.

Zackrison, R. E., & Freedman, A. (2003). Some reasons why consulting interventions fail. *Organization Development Journal, 21*(1), 72–74.

Chapter 7

Channels for OD Marketing

Zakiya Alsadah

Contents

Strategies for Marketing OD Consulting...105
    Mission Statement and Branding 105
    Professional Associations and Events...105
    Marketing OD Services at Professional Conferences.............................106
        Activity: Develop Your Own Strategic Plan for Marketing OD
        at Professional Conferences 107
    Publications...107
    Charity Goodwill 108
Social Networking and Referrals...108
    Follow-Up 109
Social Media..110
    YouTube..110
    Blogs...111
    Social Networking..111
        Facebook...111
        WhatsApp..112
        Instagram...113
        Twitter 113
        LinkedIn 114
    Activity: Create an Effective Marketing Message on Social Media 114
WOM Marketing 115

When WOM Marketing Works.. 116
Activity: This Activity Guides You Step-by-Step to Create a Successful
Viral WOM in Marketing OD 116
Case Study 117
Summary 119
References 120

Engaging in marketing for organization development (OD) consulting is not as simple as marketing a product, which just requires strategic media placement. Marketing is a process engaged in to attract and retain new customers while keeping old ones. Some companies spend millions in advertising to interest people in their products. Today, people are less inclined to believe in or be attracted to advertised products because they feel that marketers do not value their brains and opinions (Sernovitz, 2006). Further, social media and cell phones have become major advertising tools by making it possible to talk about products any time, all of the time. Therefore, as an OD consultant, you need to reach people, interest them in your services, and give them reasons to talk about your services. This requires developing the ability to craft powerful marketing messages that represent you and your experiences (Rogers, 2001). However, the critical point is to choose an adequate carrier to separate the message.

Since having business in the OD consulting field depends primarily on building and maintaining strong relationships, tools are provided in this chapter to enable OD consultants to determine the optimal marketing channels for their services. This chapter begins with a definition of the concepts used here and then highlights the importance of customizing your marketing message to suit your targeted clients—a case study serves as an example. The chapter will emphasize recent marketing channels used to reach new prospective clients. First, a wide range of social media may be used, either via informal social networks such as Twitter, blogs, and mobile apps that show the personal and human side of the consultant or through formal channels such as LinkedIn. In addition, the chapter focuses on the power of word-of-mouth (WOM) marketing and offers consultants tips for crafting powerful marketing messages.

Contribution to the Book

This chapter is the starting point in obtaining clients. It provides tools to boost marketing strategies and ensure that you benefit from the new market. Therefore, contacting people through marketing channels will take you to

the next step—communicating with prospective clients with the goal of closing the sale cycle.

Strategies for Marketing OD Consulting

OD consulting differs from other types of consulting. This consulting
approach collects ideas from people and helps them develop solutions and
plans by themselves. Sometimes, it is difficult to convince people to accept
this approach. Many view this process like that involved in medical consulting, where the doctor diagnoses the root cause of an illness and recom-
mends a medicine to the patient. In OD consulting, clients need guidance
in setting up their plans to solve their problems. It sometimes takes time to
convince a potential client to hire an OD consultant. Sometimes, what opens
the door is access to the right marketing channels. Therefore, it is better to
have a marketing strategy that utilizes new methods of contacting customers
and helps them solve their problems.

Mission Statement and Branding

Nowadays, many organizations post their information on the web (except
for confidential information, of course). A consulting company can review
organizations' missions and vision statements and suggest improvements
or changes. A consulting company can obtain a contract if it successfully
proposes modifications to mission and vision statements. If it impresses
the client, it may get referrals to others in the same industry or economic
sector.

Professional Associations and Events

Professionals can join well-known associations to connect with other
professionals who might become potential customers. Joining associations such as the Society for Human Resource Management, Organization
Development Network, and Association for Talent Development may help
members connect with people from all over the world already known in
their field. Members may join a community of practice within an association. Also, members can join a delegation or a chapter where they can
meet other professionals periodically during monthly meetings, which offer

opportunities to make presentations or propose partnerships with other consultants. Many benefits and networking opportunities can be gained from attending conferences. Contacts can be turned into business relationships. Joining professional associations and attending events and conferences can lead to business partnerships—this takes time but is necessary to longevity and success.

Marketing OD Services at Professional Conferences

- Business exhibits: once you set up your consulting firm, participating in a business exhibit can boost your brand. You can use the exhibit to attract more visitors by showing your approach to OD consultation. This may be accomplished via a small fun simulation that encourages visitors to ask more questions about OD and your consultation services. If you invested in a conference business exhibit, take advantage of your visitors. Build relationships with potentials and exchange business cards. Use their presence to ask them questions about your brand and how it could be more attractive to them.
- Relationship building: Conferences are the best place to meet with people who share your interests or offer the same services. Have your business cards handy all the time and save business cards you get from prospects. Remember that OD consulting business depends on the way people perceive you as an expert. Create opportunities to talk with people and grow your social network. Finally, practice your elevated speech.
- Presenting: Prepare intelligently if you will present at a conference. Let people know that you will present at a conference by posting on your LinkedIn, Facebook, and Twitter accounts. Create an event using social media and invite people to attend. The content and delivery are equally important. The more people attracted to your presentation, the more likely they are to become prospects and join your network. Therefore, when preparing your presentation, attend and observe bright OD consultants' sessions and focus on what attracted people's attention during their delivery. Then, you can work on improving your presenting strategy to be more appealing.

Activity: Develop Your Own Strategic Plan for Marketing OD at Professional Conferences

In the left column, you have been provided with some marketing strategies; in the right column, write your plan for marketing.

Marketing Strategy	*Your Plan*
Business Exhibit	
Business Card Exchange	
Build Relationships	
Presenting	

Publications

Different publications may be used by OD consultants as a marketing tool. After a consulting company engages in work for a company, it may wish to request permission to feature its work on behalf of the company in a magazine or other periodical and in its marketing materials and efforts. Further, OD consulting organizations may maintain connections with clients and prospects by producing and distributing monthly newsletters. The newsletter should include tips for clients, success stories, latest achievements of the organization, and future projects. Also, add a section on strategies and tools that convince readers of the need for and efficiency of the OD approach. This is an effective way to remind others of the services provided by your organization.

Another method of heightening awareness of your OD services is the publication of books on OD. Books can help you in two ways. First, they demonstrate your knowledge of the OD field. The more books you publish, the more you convince your readers of the value of your approach, skills, and abilities. When they need an OD intervention, they will think of you first. Second, people looking for OD consultants often go to Amazon and read customer reviews of OD books. Have your current customers, family members, and friends support you by expressing opinions of your OD books and appraising your knowledge and skills as an OD practitioner and author.

Charity Goodwill

Community services can grow OD consultants' business in several ways. These efforts give back to your community and market your services at the same time. Donations increase your clients' trust and loyalty. Your donation may include free or reduced cost consultation to charities. You can donate products to the charity that then uses your name and organization logo at social events. You can ask the charity to promote your name to the community or mention your contribution in its monthly newsletter (Polevoi, 2012; Stephenson & Thurman, 2007). This will further increase recognition of your brand. By engaging in these events and works, you will have opportunities to network with other donors. Attending a charity's annual meeting is another opportunity to win new clients. As we said, OD consulting is relationship based—the larger your network, the better your chances to increase your business.

Charities offer you many ways to market your brand locally. Use the following steps to help you create a plan for utilizing local charities. In the right column, develop your plan to utilize the charities in your community.

Identify local charities in your community	
Find your budget for donation	
Contact charities to see whether upcoming events require sponsorship or support	
Provide your OD consulting services, and indicate your willingness to help in their committee meetings for free	
Attend fundraising events and network with community members; give your business card and get theirs	
Strengthen your relationships with charities' boards because they have local influence and can promote the OD approach; ask them to promote you to the community in their newsletter	

Social Networking and Referrals

Networking is still the most effective marketing tool in consulting. Engagement in networking creates strong personal relationships with clients and prospective clients. The most important element in networking is to be self-aware of your marketing goals and what you are trying to accomplish by networking, which is to gain new contacts. Attend professional and social events and activities and remember to be an active listener. Listen to what people need and want, ask them questions, and interest them in you. OD practitioners attending professional events can maximize the benefits of their attendance by

- Active listening—people feel comfortable with those who listen to them. Take advantage of the opportunity to listen to collect information about people's needs, analyze any verbal messages, and observe body language to come to a correct conclusion about the story told. Then, offer your help and care for them.
- Develop your question-asking skills. The OD effort depends on the ability to ask leading questions to reach win–win results—this can be practiced when meeting people at social networking events.
- Avoid playing with your electronic devices so those with whom you come into contact feel you welcome their interaction.
- Your business card can bring you new clients. Always carry business cards with you and hand them to people you meet in any social or professional event. Give them extra for their friends because you don't know who may be your next client (Stephenson & Thurman, 2007).

Follow-Up

After each networking event and exchange of business cards, immediately follow up with prospective clients by sending e-mail, faxes, and/or letters, or making phone calls. Following up is critical in starting and maintaining business relationships. Call people you have met and mention how pleased you were to talk with them. Remind them of your services and how they can benefit from your expertise. Then show your desire for continued engagement by setting an appointment to further discuss a professional relationship (Hayden, 2007).

After each successful consultation project, ask your clients to refer you to their friends or other businesses. You can create a referral form that can be handed to your clients at the end of projects. In addition, you can set an exchange referral agreement with businesses with which you worked—you will refer their services and they will refer your consulting skills. Referrals bring you business (Berg, 1998).

Social Media

Communication in the twenty-first century has made a huge shift from traditional methods to a greater use of social media. Today, people, especially younger generations, prefer to connect, communicate, and socialize using social media programs. They use social media to find friends, express opinions, and search for businesses. Organizations can't ignore the impact of social media on their business in reaching customers and showing products. Businesses of all sizes should take advantage of the technology explosion. According to the 2014 social media marketing industry report, 92% of participating businesses said that social media is important for their business, and 97% used social media in marketing (Stelzner, 2014). Many maintain several accounts in each form of social media to stay updated and connected with their customers (Saravanakumar & SuganthaLakshmi, 2012).

Social media provides OD consultants with a powerful and cost-effective marketing tool for building their brand. Social media works as a showroom for their expertise and capabilities to potential customers. OD consultants may showcase their skills using different social media platforms. For example, YouTube may show a real-life OD intervention. Other social media channels include Blogs, Facebook, WhatsApp, Instagram, Twitter, and LinkedIn—each of these mediums is discussed here.

YouTube

YouTube is the world's largest video site and the second largest search engine. Your YouTube videos could go viral if you put effort into them. Most videos cause people to become curious about what's shown there, resulting in brand familiarity. The Korean song "Gangnam Style" is an example of a viral video with more than one billion viewers from all around the world—the dance has been practiced in different countries and cultures. YouTube is the best place to market your services if you use it strategically, such as by starting your own OD consulting channel. However, to get the most out of YouTube, you have to create interesting videos that catch viewers' attention and drive them to subscribe to your channel. Be able to do video editing, composition, and networking, or you can hire someone to help you in doing your videos (Scott, 2013; Walker, 2015). To increase the number of viewers, use fun and creative approaches in your videos, such as cartoon characters or funny characters.

Blogs

Blogs are written by people passionate about a subject. It is your own space through which to express your ideas and showcase yourself as an expert in consulting (Scott, 2013). For OD consultants, stretch your thinking and use this space to post information about successful projects that may interest prospective clients. Encourage discussions by asking questions. You can design your blog to reflect your personal side and mix it with the essence of your profession—come up with an attractive site that shows your passion and hard work in OD consulting. Gain potential customers' loyalty by highlighting evidence of your work ethics. This will lead new clients to follow you, and perhaps to refer your business.

Tips for OD practitioners

1. Choose an attractive name for your blog; it should reflect your OD profession and your personal name.
2. Choose an attractive title for your post that reflects the main points of the content.
3. The focus of the content should always reflect your niche in OD consulting.
4. Provide tips for clients to solve a problem or to deal with a business issue.
5. Point to your social media accounts and add the blog link to your social media accounts.
6. Add success stories using the OD approach to influence your followers.

Social Networking

Facebook

Approximately 757 million active daily users are on Facebook, according to a January 2014 report (Manarang, 2015). Many may be potential customers for your business. It is sometimes a good idea to reflect your interest and business in your social activities. According to the same report, 54% of participants found it the best network for business marketing. However, only 43% found Facebook marketing to be effective (Stelzner, 2014).

To make the best use of social media and especially Facebook, you need to know what it offers you in growing your business and network. Facebook has many features that may be utilized by OD consultants. First, decide if your account is personal or only for business because this is a critical point to consider. If it is personal, a feature makes this account unsearchable. If you share your personal life with your friends and family, use this feature so your potential customers will find only your business account and stay away from your personal life. Create a public account that reflects you as a person and your business and add your friends. Remember that your friends have other friends who could be prospective customers.

Tips for OD Practitioners Using Facebook

- Take advantage of the post feature, which allows friends to see and comment on your post and may attract potential clients.
- Develop a comprehensive plan for marketing your business on Facebook. The nature of the business and the services you offer will govern your posts. Your niche in OD should be there in every post. Design them to talk about you and send positive messages about your organization.
- To engage your potential customers, be creative and innovative. Try to engage the human part of your customers (OD focuses on the humanity of participants after all), so they become attached emotionally to you—this can lead to long-term relationships with customers. Having a variety of types of posts can satisfy different customers. Studies have shown that posts of an emotional nature receive 33% more comments than other normal posts do (Barell, 2013; Trusov, Bucklin, & Pauwels, 2009).
- Keep the post professional, short, and concise. Add an attractive image—posts with images get 39% more comments than do posts without images (Barell, 2013).
- Encourage discussions about OD on your page by asking questions or posting a current event or topic related to your services. But be smart in choosing the right time to post—that is, identify the hours in which most of your friends are online. You can post educational articles about OD, short videos of you talking, and practical OD tools for clients to use.
- Add your social media-sharing plug-in to make it easier for your page's visitors to share your page with their friends. Also, direct your website visitors to your social media sites and personal Facebook page by adding their icons at the top of the website.

WhatsApp

WhatsApp is a mobile app that can be installed on cell phones and recently on computers. It allows users to chat and share voice, video, and written messages. Normal users can create groups of people of 100—family, organizations, or friends. Everyone in the group can see each other's phone numbers and personal status and profile image. They can interact with each other and participate in any discussion. However, users can create a larger group (service), such as a community service that anyone in the community can be added to for a fee. Subscribers get the same messages from the service at the same time. The special thing about this service is that no one in a group knows who is participating in the service. According to academia .edu (2015), around the world, people are using and spending more time on WhatsApp than any other social media, including Facebook and Twitter, with 450 million users. Marketing in WhatsApp is viral (Pune, 2015). However, in consulting, you need to make it more professional. If you are new to business, you can reach your current customers with your services using videos or a proficiently designed message to promote you and forward the message to their contacts. Messages through WhatsApp will travel across countries, so be careful about your brand; you can get one million customers or ruin your brand. A more professional strategy may be to use a trusted and credible community service in your area (if it has one) in sending your ad to participants, and don't forget to add your name, website, phone number, and Facebook page at the tail of the WhatsApp message.

Instagram

Instagram is one of the most popular mobile applications, with 300 million users in 2014 (Constine, 2014). This service allows you to post pictures and short videos in your account. As an OD consultant, you can follow your potential customers and other recognized OD practitioners. Use your account to show your knowledge and experience by participating in OD discussions, so others notice you. Or use your account to post your services or create a topic for discussion and mention your potential clients to your post to participate. In addition, Instagram allows you to tape-record up to 60 seconds videos; it is short, but it's good for offering OD advice. Using Instagram wisely can actively market your OD service, and increase your customers.

Twitter

Twitter is a social media application that allows users to share their ideas and thoughts in only 140 characters. In 2014, Twitter followed Instagram in numbers of monthly active users by 288 million users (Twitter.com,

2015). People are using this website for different purposes. Some are using it for news, while others visit for education, entertainment, and advertisement. Some people tweet about their favorite book or what they are reading right now. Others tweet quotes from some of the books they have read.

As an OD consultant, create a network of OD consulting professionals and participate in discussions and express yourself and talent in consulting through your tweets to target customers. Also, post the latest books you read that relate to your area and suggest new ones. Potential customers are more likely to find you when searching tweets related to consulting.

LinkedIn

LinkedIn is more formal than other social media applications. For marketing consulting services, it gives you a guide for building a brand that may help you to do better than your competitors. It offers choices for business owners as they build strong profiles and connect with the right people; it also allows them to grow deep relationships by posting valuable content (LinkedIn.com).

How OD Consultants Use LinkedIn for Marketing

First step: Create a page for your organization and design it so it offers insights into who you are and describes OD. Upload good videos of you facilitating an OD effort and add links to any publications you have about OD.

Second step: Add the brightest OD practitioners to your network and like and comment on their post to show your name.

Third step: Join professional OD groups. There are many OD groups, so join as many as you can handle and become involved in discussions that present you as an influential OD consultant. Start a discussion or answer questions in your groups, and don't forget to have your organization's page address at the end of your discussion participation.

Fourth step: Ask recognized OD practitioners to recommend you to give you more credibility.

Activity: Create an Effective Marketing Message on Social Media

Advertising a product via media usually requires following certain steps, such as using attractive pictures, findings ways to be creative, and demonstrating product functions that would attract customers. However, when engaging in marketing consulting, many of these steps may seem inapplicable because we are talking about human services that depend on relationships.

Your consulting marketing message is the first step in establishing business relationships with customers. People spend little time reading marketing messages and may omit details. Therefore, whether communicating via mass or digital social media, your message should be concise and convey all the elements needed to ensure to target customer buy-in (LinkedIn Small Business, 2015).

Use the following formula to practice writing an effective message for social media.

The left column provides you with the essential elements of an effective marketing message. In the right column is a space to create your customized marketing message related to OD services you provide.

You used the exact name of your services in your marketing message	
Stated the need of your services	
Stated who is your target customer	
Why your services are unique	
The message is attractive, and can catch the potential customer attention.	
You included your contact information	
Your are using the best marketing channel for this messages	

WOM Marketing

People love to talk about just about everything. In the past they talked to their friends, families, and neighbors. Now they talk with everyone including strangers from other countries on their blogs or via comments on websites (Sernovitz, 2006). They express their opinion about the smallest thing to the biggest topic or issue you can imagine. In consultation, people still talk about their good and bad experiences with consultants. If clients like you and your services don't go the extra mile in advertising and marketing your products because they will give you a boost and let everybody know you.

WOM marketing seems simple. Yes, it is simple and complicated at the same time. It is easy to get people to talk but you want to make you and your services appealing enough to talk about. Your goal is to be promoted by your customers to their friends and followers, not to ruin your brand (Fang, 2014; Sernovitz, 2006).

When WOM Marketing Works

The Word of Mouth Marketing Association defines WOM marketing as "the art and science of building active, mutually beneficial consumer-to-consumer and consumer-to-marketer communication" (Sernovitz, 2006, p. 3). WOM can be a fire that burns all your efforts because you have upset customers or a rocket ship that takes your name and business to the top. It reflects how your customers have received your services. People need a reason to talk, so your job as a consultant is to make your customers feel great about you and your services so they want to talk about you to their friends and other people and recommend you to them. In consulting, it is a challenge to get a customer out of thinking in a traditional advertising mode because you are talking about yourself. Your customers are your advertisers. Most of your business results from colleagues' recommendations and referrals—potential clients may be more likely to hear about you if current and previous customers talk about their experiences with you. However, if you are a victim of negative WOM, especially on social media, think of it as an opportunity to polish your picture and show you care about your clients. Contact the upset customer and try to understand what went wrong and satisfy him or her, and you may win him or her over enough to lead him or her to recommend your business. Otherwise, having your mistakes pointed out to you will lead you to improve yourself.

Activity: This Activity Guides You Step-by-Step to Create a Successful Viral WOM in Marketing OD

Steps in crafting a viral WOM for OD consultants

- Identify the target market segments you want to reach.
- Identify people who can talk about you in the media and with colleagues' old clients, book reviewers, and friends.

■ Give them a reason to talk about your services—develop a message to send out that indicates how you compare to others (e.g., comparative look at your services vs. your competitors), describes your communication style and services, points out your best qualities (e.g., honest, skillful), and lists your successes in addressing others' business problems or needs (Sernovitz, 2006; Stephenson & Thurman, 2007).

■ If they are posting on social media, participate in the conversations and address questions that arise.

■ Address any negative feedback quickly and turn it into an opportunity to learn and develop.

■ Have a trustful relationship with your current and potential clients. Your business ethics should be stated clearly for customers because people will not refer others to a business they don't trust.

■ Keep monitoring the conversations, and maintain and strengthen any new relationships so you can get more people to talk about you.

Case Study

Alex launched a consulting company during his PhD study in 2004. He used his home as an office and his home address was on his business cards. Since it would be difficult for people to stop by his business, he tried to market his services in different ways. He started by knocking on local businesses' doors. He visited businesses in town. Nothing worked the first year. He asked two local stores to discuss their reasons for not hiring him to do consulting work. He assumed that the first reason he was not being hired after several visits to local businesses was his newness in the consulting business—people didn't want to risk signing a contract with him. He thought of different channels for letting people hear about his services and learning to trust him so he would get a contract. He joined local community groups and participated in some of them. Also, he offered his services for free to one of the charities in his town. During his free service there, charity members came to learn about his work and expertise. His ability to help that charity to create a new vision and mission increased his reputation in his community. Those affiliated with that charity talked about him with their friends, creating a good marketing channel for him.

Alex was facing two challenges as a new consultant. The first challenge was to gain customers' trust. The second challenge was his use of a different consulting approach. Initially, it was difficult for him to convince people to sign a contract with him, but after his successful experience with the charity, he could get more contracts. Therefore, he depended on WOM in gaining business and having new customers. After his graduation in May 2008, he got a job as an instructor at a well-known university on the south coast of the United States. During his lectures at that school, he noticed that students were always using their smartphones. They spent many hours on their phones. He was looking for a way to market his services and get more customers. So, he started by creating a Facebook page and added his friends. He realized that people were talking about their social life, posting their dinner pictures, or adding pictures from their trips but no one from his network was posting something about business. He then tried to expand his Facebook network to include other friends from his friends contact list but focused this time on those who mentioned in their profiles their profession and who posted pictures from their business meetings. Also, he found people who posted products for sale. He sent invitations to his clients. Their friends also added his Facebook page. This helped him to expand his network. How could he have used his Facebook page to be more business oriented and more efficient? He hired two young employees with experience in social media. They developed a plan to attract more customers using a new marketing channel. They used Alex's company mission and goals and how his company helped other clients to achieve better results. They obtained questions from others and comments from former clients. Some of the former clients commented about their privacy and so did not want their names posted on Facebook. Also, some new potential customers might not want to show others that they are looking for help from a consultant. They were afraid their employees would learn about their future plans—how was Alex to handle this issue? How could they protect their customers' privacy but continue doing business using Facebook?

Alex's team thought about using Twitter as a marketing channel for their company. They started by following some of the famous consulting organizations already on Twitter. Also, they followed organizations that might become potential customers. At the same time, people followed Alex's consulting company. In the first month, Alex's company followed 2000 accounts, including publishers, organizations, consulting companies, associations, and other individuals—either old customers or people who had found Alex's company an interesting account to follow. Alex's team began tweeting 20 tweets every day and retweeting around 30 tweets every day. Sometimes, they repeated some of their good tweets several times a week or month. Sometimes, they gave advice through their Twitter account or posed questions to followers or sent links about studies they were conducting and tried to recruit participants. They increased their advertising services without paying too much money for an advertising firm. As a consultant, can you think of a way to utilize Twitter in a more efficient way?

What other social media websites could Alex use to advertise his company's services?

- Are social media websites useful marketing channels for consulting associations?
- Do you agree with Alex's strategy of using social media as a marketing channel? Why?
- What are the challenges of using social media as a marketing channel?
- Can you relate a successful business story that involves social media?

Summary

OD marketing strategies can be a challenge for consultants, especially as they begin their journey in consulting. These challenges are due in part to OD being a service that is not "touchable" as a product and in part to potential clients' not knowing whether they can trust your business. It is about building relationships with potential clients and maintaining them. Clients will not be convinced of your ability to help them by seeing your advertisements on traditional media. However, consultants may utilize several marketing channels to build a relationship of trust with potential clients. In this chapter, we discussed different traditional and current methods for helping you shape your brand and get more business.

The first marketing strategy is to publish books and attend conferences that relate to your area of expertise. This strategy is guaranteed to reserve you a place among consulting professionals. In addition, we discussed the impact of social networking and attending professional and social events on obtaining more business—don't forget the impact of making donations to charity in polishing your brand. Meeting new prospective clients at social events does not mean you have engaged them in your business but requires you to do more work in following up repeatedly until you close the sale cycle.

The major part of this chapter looked at the effect of social media on marketing OD consulting. Most businesses today are using social media to reach their customers. Social media is a great marketing channel for OD consultants because it is based on socializing and building social relationships that lead to business, because relationships are the easiness of consulting. Finally, WOM marketing should be considered—this chapter contains an activity to help consultants craft an effective message for social networks.

References

Barell, R. (2013). Using Facebook science to get more engagement (info graphic). Retrieved from http://www.bitrebels.com/social/facebook-science-engagement -infographic/

Berg, B. (1998). *Endless referrals: Network your everyday contacts into sale*. New York: McGraw-Hill.

Constine, J. (2014). Instagram hits 300 million monthly users to surpass Twitter. Keep it real with verified badges. Retrieved from: http://techcrunch.com/2014 /12/10/not-a-. Get people talkiad/

Fang, Y. (2014). Beyond the credibility of electronic word of mouth: Exploring eWOM adoption on social networking sites from affective and curiosity perspectives. *International Journal of Electronic Commerce, 18*(3), 67–102. doi:10.2753/JEC1086-4415180303

Hayden, C. J. (2007). *Get clients now* (2nd ed.). San Francisco: American Management Association.

LinkedIn Small Business. (2015) Marketing. Retrieved from: https://smallbusiness .linkedin.com/small-business-marketing

Manarang, R. (2015). Effective Facebook marketing strategies for business. Retrieved from: http://roelcreative.com/effective-facebook-marketing-strategy/

Polevoi, L. (2012). Charitable giving is good for your business. Retrieved from: http:// quickbooks.intuit.com/r/money/charitable-giving-is-good-for-your-business/

Pune, I. (2015). *Can WhatsApp be a new digital marketing tool*. Retrieved from: https://www.academia.edu/9466433/Can_WhatsApp_Be_Used_As_a_New _Digital_Marketing_Tool

Rogers, S. C. (2001). *Marketing strategies, tactics, and techniques: A handbook for practitioners*. Westport, CT: Quorum Books.

Saravanakumar, M., & SuganthaLakshmi, T. (2012). Social media marketing. *Life Science Journal, 9*(4), 4444–4451.

Scott, D. M. (2013). *The new rules of marketing and PR* (4th ed.). Hoboken, NJ: John Wiley & Sons, Inc.

Sernovitz, A. (2006). *Word of mouth marketing: How smart companies get people talking*. Chicago, IL: Kaplan Pub.

Stelzner, M. A. (2014). Social media marketing industry report. *Social Media Examiner, 41*.

Stephenson, J., & Thurman, C. (2007). *Ultimate small business marketing guide: 1500 great marketing tricks that will drive your business through the roof*. Irvine, CA: Entrepreneur Press.

Trusov, M., Bucklin, R. E., & Pauwels, K. (2009). Effects of word-of-mouth versus traditional marketing: Findings from an internet social networking site. *Journal of Marketing, 73*(5), 90–102.

Twitter.com (2015). Twitter usage. Retrieved from: https://about.twitter.com/company

Walker, T. (2015). *The no hype guide to video marketing on YouTube*. Retrieved from: http://www.convinceandconvert.com/content-marketing/the-no-hype-guide-to -video-marketing-on-youtube/

Chapter 8

Communication Planning and Branding

Azadeh Omrani-Kermani

Contents

Case Study 124
Communication Aligned with Branding......................................124
Expertise Meets Target Market..125
Communication Comes First..125
Keys to Communication...125
First Meeting 127
Keep in Touch 129
Communication Tools for Internal OD Professional 129
Referrals 130
The Branding Concept..130
Protecting the Brand 130
Summary 131
References 131

In this chapter, we will discuss organization development (OD) consultant communication and branding for both internal and external OD consultants. We will illustrate the relationship between communication and branding while investigating how the field can improve communication. Then we will introduce tools that will help communication strategies. We will illustrate how to take advantage of them from your first communication effort. We will consider an external OD consultant. Also, we will refer to the tools and techniques of the internal consultant. Finally, we will talk about branding concepts and how to develop and sustain them.

Case Study

Chris founded an OD consulting company. He advertised his wide variety of consulting services in magazines, as well as mailing brochures and newsletters. Unfortunately, he did not receive any responses from his marketing efforts. As a result, his OD consulting services was a failure.

Bob is an individual OD consultant, who is successful in his career development. An example of his success is contacting organizations and presenting his services. One of his strengths is discovering the problematic issues within the companies, then he provides practical solutions to these issues. As a result, the organizations that used his OD consultation are satisfied with the services he provides.

What is the difference between these two individuals? This chapter will review effective communication tools and explore how to build OD consulting brands and bring them to the market.

Communication Aligned with Branding

Consultation as a service industry is an intangible product. Communication style can indicate the quality of services in a customer's mind (Berry & Seltman, 2007). The quality of the service establishes its brand image and illustrates the expected experience with service providers. Define the target market and communication strategy carefully. To find out these two important aspects of your business, try to respond to these questions:

- What is your expertise?
- What are your services and products? Workshops? Training? Books? Consulting sessions?
- Do you offer performance consulting or OD consulting?
- Who are your ideal prospective customers?
- Where can you find your customers?
- How can you identify customers' problems to offer consulting services?
- How can you introduce yourself and your consulting services in 30 seconds?

- What is your competitive advantage that will attract customers to your services rather than them going to your competitors?
- Where can you contact customers? In what events? By telephone or in person?

Let's address the most important question: What is your expertise?

Expertise Meets Target Market

Select your area(s) of expertise from Table 8.1, the wide range of OD intervention options.

Once you have selected an option(s), you need to further develop your expertise in these particular area(s). Keep in mind to focus on several (two or three) of these option(s). This is the best means to become a knowledgeable OD consultant. As a result of this expertise, you are creating a brand to market to organizations who need your expertise in these area(s).

Communication Comes First

The beginning of all business relationships starts with good communication. As a result, mutual influence exists between the parties. As a consultant, continuously look for ways to develop your relationship with your customers. Also continue to discover new ways to add value to your OD consulting services for your customers. An example of this is developing the business relationship into a legitimate friendship. Through this relationship, you can discover the customers' issues in order to offer better solutions than through the consultant to client relationship. The most important means to discover the clients' issues is through casual conversation. The use of open-ended questions without offering solutions will accomplish this end.

Keys to Communication

Communication starts with contact. As a consultant, you can collect the contact information for various organizations through attending conferences, seminars' and Chamber of Commerce events, etc. At these events, briefly introduce yourself and your field of expertise to the representatives from

Table 8.1 OD Interventions

OD Intervention	Communication Issues
Counseling/coaching	Find the top managers and ask for their issues in the company. Try to give hints through open-ended questions.
Training	Find out what skills and training the organization needs. Determine if you can provide the training yourself, or if you can refer the organization to another competent OD consultant to provide the necessary training that the organization requires.
Job description	Evaluate each job description and determine whether the responsibilities fit its title.
Performance appraisal systems	If the managers are concerned about the performance and productivity of employees, then you can propose an OD approach in relationship to improve performance and productivity.
Life and career planning	Discover the employees' concerns toward their career and life goals and offer consulting according to those specific needs.
Team building	Teams are always important in projects, and their performance can impact the whole organization's success. You can always inquire about the teams' effectiveness and productivity.
Unit goal setting	Determine the unit goal setting based upon the desired productivity of the team.
Conflict management	A strategy to identify conflict among team members and provide a resolution for better team members' performance.
Cross-functional training	Figure out if two different units of an organization need special training to effectively communicate and function together.
Work redesign	The job definition is redesigned.
Quality and productivity systems	Organizations who are not satisfied with their productivity and quality throughout their system.
Customer service development	The focus of employees to improve the effectiveness and efficiency of customer service.

Note: Distinguish if you can provide services regarding the issues and your field of expertise.

the various organizations. Prepare a brief and effective description of OD consulting for those who are not aware of what OD consulting is. Also ask for their contact information. The more contact information you gather, the more business you will generate. The following week, contact the organizations by telephone or in person. Briefly introduce yourself and your expertise, remind them where you met their representatives. Request for a meeting with the chief executive officer (CEO) and/or human resource (HR) manager to discuss how your OD services can benefit their organization needs. At the end of your presentation, leave some time for questions and answers. Based upon the questions asked, look for any possible concerns and issues that you can address through your consulting services.

First Meeting

The first meeting should take place in person (face to face). If not, a telephone call or the use of Skype would be an ideal alternative for the first meeting. During this meeting, focus on the client's concerns while elaborating on your services that will be valuable and useful to his or her organization.

During the first meeting, you may discover that the CEO and HR manager might not know of the OD approaches. As a result, be prepared to give a presentation concerning the OD approach and how it may apply to the organization's issues. This presentation should reflect your field of expertise. Listed here are the most frequent questions asked about the OD approach:

■ What is OD?
■ What is OD for?
■ What are the practices of OD?
■ What is the return of investment of OD?
■ What other companies have applied OD?

While these questions are important from the client's perspective, you can avoid the client asking them if you provide a complete and simple definition for your OD approach and services. This way, the client does not ask needless questions. Table 8.2 provides you with some OD terms that are easy to understand without any questions needed to clarify them to your client.

These simplified terms can make your first meeting more productive while addressing your client's needs more easily.

Table 8.2   Simplified OD Terms

OD Term	Easy Term
OD approach	Change management
Talent management	Talent finding
Succession management	Talent retention
Competency modeling	Finding talents for positions
Job description	Job description

Note: Simplify professional OD terms into simple, unquestionable concepts.

The following strategies will assist you with communicating with your client, concerning his or her issues and needs (Djavanshir & Agresti, 2007):

■ Discover the client's expectations, interests, need, and perspectives during your first meeting. This can be done through open-ended questions; listen carefully to his or her responses to the questions you have asked him or her. Determine what services can meet the client's needs.
■ Be aware of the client's sociocultural mindset and values. Avoid conducting yourself in a disrespectful manner. Take time to educate yourself regarding the organization's social/cultural norms and mores.
■ As best as possible, try to establish an informal conversation and communication style with your client. As a result, this will help you to find out the deeper issues with less resistance from your client.

Be prepared to offer your client multiple options. Once you have gathered sufficient information regarding the issues facing the organization, then you can properly draft a proposal with the input from the CEO and HR manager which will solve these issues. Among your questions, figure out how much the issue costs for the organization. One of the questions you must consider while addressing these issues is how much the company saves versus the expense of not solving the issue. At the conclusion of your first meeting, try to reach an agreement about how your service can benefit to the customer's organization.

After the first meeting, you should have an overall view of the issues facing the company and how much they are costing it. Discover the client's expectations for solving the organization's issues. Then you can prepare a proposal accordingly. This can be done through listening and observing your client's behavior, expectations, thoughts, and values. Also, you can offer your client a free consultation session or a brief workshop, if they believe it is necessary for their organization.

Keep in Touch

The cost to acquire a new customer is 6 to 10 times more than keeping existing customers. This is the primary reason for staying in constant contact with your present customers. There are many ways to present your current services to your clients. For example, the conventional way of presenting the latest services to your customers is by sending out cards, e-mails, and text messages for their anniversaries and birthdays. This is a brief, effective, and simple way to stay in the clients' mind.

Another example of reminding your clients about these services is to send out online newsletters at least twice a week. This newsletter can include the most recent articles in your field of expertise, recent OD events, and your organization's latest news.

The newest way to keep in continuous contact with your clients is through the use of social media, such as Facebook pages and groups, Twitter, YouTube, etc. The advantage of social media is that the interaction is based on direct feedback and testimonials. Also, it allows you to manage your OD consulting interaction with your clients over Facebook.

Communication Tools for Internal OD Professional

Internal OD professionals should be in contact with every section of the organization. They should participate in all meetings related to the issues in the organization; they should make an inquiry about all aspects of their activities through the use of a survey.

It is important that they can stay in contact with the other sections of the organization. This can be done through posting the recent findings in OD and HR bulletin boards. In addition, inform other sections about your recent activities. Also, you can provide occasional workshops for exploring the issues. Take time to closely talk about their concerns and issues.

Referrals

Either external or internal OD consulting must create its future projects from the current projects. For example, current clients can provide future referrals to other organizational sections within the company. Or they can refer you to other organizations who can use your services because they have similar issues. As a result of these clients' referrals and testimonials, future projects should be generated for your OD consulting business. Lastly, always request a referral from a current client for future projects.

The Branding Concept

In simple terms, branding in the service industry is about a customer's experience with a service provider. Branding can be divided into two categories: tangible and intangible. The tangible tools for communicating a brand message are advertising, brand name, logo, websites, employee uniforms, and facility design. Furthermore, the main forms of external brand communication are publicity and word of mouth communication established via Internet blogging, message boards, personal websites, newsletters, and social media. These forms of communication provide brand awareness, although maybe not in the desired manner. Possible customers need an independent and unbiased source of information to determine whether or not to hire your OD consulting services.

The customers' experience is a cumulative process between the customer and the service organization. The customers' experience is foundational for building a brand image. For example, a poor brand image cannot be improved by advertising (Djavanshir & Agresti, 2007). Unlike some industries, the branding for OD consulting services derives its reputation from the clients' experience. A successful brand brings you more business. Once you have achieved this, maintaining the brand image is a necessity. This can be achieved through completing projects in a timely and cost-effective fashion for your clients. In the end, this will save your clients money and time while increasing the value of your brand equity.

Protecting the Brand

The best way to protect your brand is to define and distinguish your values through continuing to provide quality services to your clients. For example,

Berry and Seltman (2007) state, "The values of the service provider directly influence the quality and value of their service."

Remember, for any marketing and branding activity, there is always something more to be done. Do not make the mistake of thinking that your brand will go on by itself. If you stop developing your brand, it becomes obsolete. To avoid this, always be thinking about new ways of developing your brand for your target market and potential customers. Branding is an ongoing process that is never done.

Summary

In this chapter, we have illustrated the importance of communication style in OD consulting. Also, we discussed the impact of communication tools on a business. Furthermore, we provided guidelines about various OD interventions regarding your field of expertise. The principals presented to you prepare you for your first contact. It is important how to conduct yourself in your first meeting with the client. The possible questions you will be asked by a client are listed in order to prepare your responses for the first meeting.

Then, we described the internal OD consultant duties on communication within the organization. Next, we talked about branding and the difference between OD consulting and other service branding. Lastly, we covered the importance of receiving referrals from current clients; how they can affect your branding was discussed too.

The final point discussed was how communication and branding is an ongoing concept. It should be continuously developed during your OD consulting business. You are always looking for efficient and effective ways to improve your branding.

References

Berry, L. L., & Seltman, K. D. (2007). Building a strong services brand: Lessons from Mayo Clinic. *Business Horizons, 50,* 199–209. doi:10.1016/j.bushor.2007.01.005

Djavanshir, G. R., & Agresti, W. W. (2007). IT consulting: Communication skills are key. *IT Professional, 9*(February 2007), 46–50. http://doi.org/10.1109/MITP.2007.15

Chapter 9

Personal Sales

Jamie Campbell

Contents

Critical Questions for Personal Sales 134
    What Is Your Product? 135
        Exercise 1: What Is Your Product? 136
    Who Are Your Customers/Clients? 136
        Exercise 2: Who Are Your Clients? 137
    Who Are Your Main Stakeholders? 137
        Exercise 3: Identify Your Main Stakeholders and Stockholders 138
    Who Are You Competing Against? 139
        Exercise 4: Who Is Your Competition? 139
    What Makes Your Services Different? 140
        Exercise 5: How Are You Different? 141
    How Are You Going to Earn Income? 142
        Exercise 6: The Formula 142
Self-Promotion 144
Presentations 147
    Structure 148
        Exercise 7: Laying the Foundation 149
    Content 149
        Introduction 150
        Information 150
        Call to Action 151
        Conclusion 152

Medium 152
Delivery 153
Proposal Writing 154
Client Management 155
References 156

As an organization development (OD) professional, you develop training and programming for clients. However, have you considered the needs of your most important client? Who is this incredible client we are speaking about? The answer is simple, it's YOU! You are the most important client you will have. Remember, people who market professional services rarely fail due to lack of information about effective sales and marketing techniques (Hayden, 2013). This chapter will give you tips to prevent failure in securing sales and growing your business.

Strategic goals, such as those we will define, not only provide direction but also provide the propulsion that enables you to move forward despite current fads in the industry (Weiss, 2009). Chapter 7 helped you craft your elevator pitch. It gave you some pointers for your presentation skills using forms of media to develop a top-notch presentation. Next, we examined how to make calls to clients who may not know of the services you can provide. Techniques to manage the client and the format for getting proposals reviewed and accepted were also examined.

This chapter will help you to market yourself as a consultant, a brand, and a business.

Critical Questions for Personal Sales

You are at a conference dinner table where you repeatedly hear an individual complain about issues happening at the company where he or she works.

What should you do?

Better yet, how do you engage this possible client?

While each conference dinner setting is different, in this (common) scenario, you have been presented with an opportunity! The individual attending this "conference" is attending for the same reasons you are: to learn new tactics, network, and find someone to help. If you are properly prepared, you may place yourself in a position to gain a new client with just a 30-second introduction.

This 30-second introduction is better known as an *elevator pitch*. The purpose of this pitch is not to introduce you to the person but you to the business. Traditionally, an elevator pitch is only a soft pitch, a marker of what your company can do for your potential client. Its time length should be only 30 to 45 seconds. That is literally the time it takes for most elevators to cover one to two floors. MacLean (2012) points out that every successful pitch must be able to concisely answer six questions:

- What is your product?
- Who are your customers/clients?
- Who are your main stakeholders?
- Who are you competing against?
- What makes your services different?
- How are you going to earn income?

Let us take these six questions apart to craft the best pitch for your business. In developing answers to these questions, the answers will change as your business expands. As a consultant, it is import to remain flexible. As your business grows, so must you!

What Is Your Product?

You are selling OD consulting. While that is actually a service, it may be regarded as a product for our purposes. This means that a service for analyzing corporate environments to improve processes, recruitment, and employee development is being offered. When crafting the answer to the question "what is your product"? you may develop points to define your area of your expertise. At this point, it is also important to craft one or two brief examples of what you can do. The keyword is *brief.* Do not give away too much information right away. It will also be important to remember the time constraints you are dealing with. This is an ideal time to craft your verbal resume (VR). Your VR should be your company name, where you are located, and your business card. When discussing your particular brand of consulting, remember that you may have to explain exactly what OD is and how it can be beneficial. Do not take for granted that your targeted client will have a complete understanding of what type of support is being offered to him or her. Providing concise explanations of what OD does for companies can help you with your follow-up conversations.

Thinking about your product? Great! WRITE IT DOWN (see Exercise 1). The more you say it, write it, and envision it, the better you can convey it.

Exercise 1: What Is Your Product?

1. Define areas of expertise
   a. _____
   b. _____
   c. _____
2. Example
   a. _____
   b. _____
3. Verbal resume
   a. _____
   b. _____

Who Are Your Customers/Clients?

To what type of customers/clients are your products and services best suited? Is there a particular part of the country they are located? Remember that clients are defined as the group or person whose purposes and needs the OD consultant serves and represents (Rothwell & Sredl, 2000). Customers are a little trickier to define. At the root, customers fit the information you provide. This information can be anything from on-site training to large-scale conference style lectures. Customers will differ from clients because they may not be the one paying for the services. Weiss takes this client–customer relationship idea one step further. He changes the terminology to *feasibility buyers* and *economic buyers*. The economic buyer is usually the person who is the decision maker, the chief executive officer, chief information officer, or chief financial officer. The feasibility buyer is usually the person who is a little further down in the command chain. Think of the coordinators, directors, and assistants—while they do not have absolute authority, they can eventually get you in front of the feasibility buyer. The keyword in the last sentence is *eventually*; once the economic buyer thinks that the information you have provided is complete, he or she then can suggest the use of your services. What this ultimately means is as the consultant, you have to not only design programs that work for the consumer but also satisfy the needs of the client. Understanding this will help you to tailor your pitch to different cooperate situations. Another important question to evaluate in this process is how big is your "ideal" client? If your ideal client has 10,000 employees who need training provided, can you do it, and can you do it well? If your ideal client only has 20 employees, can you work well in the close quarters that is the small business? Can you be available at a moment's notice? Large conglomerate or small "Mom and Pop," some of your clients may be high touch and expect you to be on site personally if a situation arises. A *high-touch client* means exactly what it sounds like. This client is very interested in having your full attention, all the time. Big issues or small ones, they expect you to handle their issues quickly. Is your organization built to handle such a demanding client? When making your initial pitch, you may not have this information in front of you, but you can get a feel for what type of attention this client will need by listening to them.

Assigning definitions to customers and clients will help you develop your pitch. It will also help keep the relationship lines between customer and client clear. A key mistake you should try to avoid is being unaware for whom you are working.

Okay, so do you know who your possible clients are? Great! WRITE IT DOWN.

Exercise 2: Who Are Your Clients?

1. Where are they?
   a. _____
   b. _____
   c. _____
2. How big are they?
   a. From _____ employees to _____ employees
3. What field(s) are they in?
   a. _____
   b. _____
   c. _____

Who Are Your Main Stakeholders?

In the Introduction, we defined who your number 1 client is. Now let's expand that circle of importance. Did you know that if you try to find a simple definition of the word *stakeholder* in Google, you get 24 million results (in Internet Explorer, it's "only" 3.2 million). What they both agree on is that a *stakeholder* has a true interest in your company and your business endeavors. So why is this important to know when giving your elevator pitch? The answer is simple, you are no longer just representing yourself. While it is your business, and the earnings of this business depend solely on your efforts, someone had to help you get started. These people are your stakeholders. Your efforts should reflect them and their needs. Which of your contacts have provided you leads? Who among your contacts provided resources for you to develop your training materials? Another important factor to understand is that the term *stakeholders* can be interchanged with *stockholders*. *Stockholders* should be considered as those persons who provide hard assets such as money and materials to support your growth. However, stockholders differ from stakeholders because stockholders want and need to see a monetary return on any investment they provide for you. Keeping your stockholders happy can be difficult, but manageable. Your ability to keep them happy begins with your successful pitch and selection of clients.

For additional information on the differences in stakeholders and stockholders, two articles that can provide some clarity are Donaldson and Preston's (1995) *The Stakeholder Theory of the Corporation: Concepts, Evidence, and Implications* and Mitchell, Agle, and Wood's *Toward a Theory of Stakeholder Identification and Salience: Defining the Principle of Who and What Really Counts.*

Exercise 3: Identify Your Main Stakeholders and Stockholders

For this exercise, review the people whom you speak with to try to secure business. Look at your top six prospects for generating business. Where do they fit on the following chart? How much time does each person need from you for a positive outcome? How many proposals do they have to see before a decision can be made?

1. Stakeholder
   a. _____
   b. _____
   c. _____
2. Stockholders
   a. _____
   b. _____
   c. _____

Who Are You Competing Against?

As you prepare to speak with different company representatives to get your business in front of their company, remember that you are not the only person trying to secure business from them. In refining your pitch, know what the consulting landscape looks like. You must understand where your competitors are entering the market. Assessing the market means you take a hard look at who is doing exactly what you do. While many groups say they are consultants, few can say they are OD consultants. Understand the size and scope of your business. Just starting out it will be difficult to compete with the larger firms. The resources at a larger firm's disposal can seem limitless. You can challenge any company for the business out there, but know what you are up against. Looking internally will also help you to define who your competition is on the open market. When you know your company's capability, it can help you to see who and what you are going up against.

Why is knowing all of this important during your elevator pitch?

Simply answered, information is power. The more you know about the landscape, the better your pitch will be. Defining your competition will help in preparing your approach to a possible client and show you what they may have already heard from a competitor. Reviewing your competition can also provide other valuable insights. It can allow you to see where you have opportunities for possible work with an outside agency. Being a consultant means that generating business is one of your primary concerns for survival. If you can get another agency's support on a job or pitch they are trying to develop, it could turn into easy revenue for your business. The current landscape can also provide you with a look into the future. What are your aspirant companies? An *aspirant company* is a company or firm that you want your firm to develop into in the future. There are certain categories that should be examined: areas such as size, volume of business, number of employees, and most importantly what is this company doing for revenue generation. These factors are all a part of what makes the company aspirational. Developing and reviewing this information as your company begins its journey can help you decide the clients you want to approach.

Exercise 4: Who Is Your Competition?

There is an old saying, *keep your friends close, but your enemies* (i.e., competitors) *closer.* Look at the current consulting landscape. What firms are your immediate competitors? What companies do you want to emulate?

Working with your peers and advanced companies, can you grow your business? In the following, write out who can hurt and help you in your professional growth. Assessing the strengths and weaknesses of both collaborators and competitors can help you to see how to position your firm in the current market.

1. Possible Competitors
   a. _____
      i. Strengths
      ii. Weakness
   b. _____
      i. Strengths
      ii. Weakness
   c. _____
      i. Strengths
      ii. Weakness
2. Possible Collaborators
   a. _____
   b. _____
   c. _____
3. Aspirant Companies
   a. _____
      i. Size
      ii. Revenue
   b. _____
      i. Size
      ii. Revenue

What Makes Your Services Different?

By surveying the landscape of the current OD consultant marketplace, you now have an idea on what competitors do that is similar to your business plan. You should evaluate what your business will be able to do differently in the same arena. Think of it this way, would you go to a general doctor for a root canal? You might, but wouldn't you want to go to a dentist who specializes in this area? The general practitioner and the dentist are both doctors, but the dentist possesses special expertise. Two doctors, yet one has a differentiator that makes him or her better for the root canal job.

Differentiators are things you can readily identify to make you stand out from the rest of the marketplace. By highlighting your differentiators, you make your abilities rise out of the noise coming from your competition. The first differentiator is that you are an OD consultant. It cannot be overstated or understated that most of your potential clients do not understand the services you can provide. Your job is to make it plain that as an OD consultant, there are benefits to hiring you as opposed to a general consultant. A general consultant cannot provide the detail and expertise in OD as you can. Think of using this example when pitching to clients. Ask your possible client this question: "Would you go to a general practitioner for a root canal?" A general practitioner is a doctor just like a dentist, but for a root canal, you want a specialist. OD consultants are specialists who can get to the specific points of a problem. This is how you can position yourself with prospective clients. Capitalizing on this is the start to exposing your array of skills to new customers. The size of your new consulting group can also be useful. Large or small, size matters to some clients; too many clients can be read as too many for Company X to be important. Too few clients could be questioned as why do they not have more, do they not know what they are doing? Be prepared for both, especially during your elevator pitch! Your practiced answers can provide your potential clients with insight on just how prepared you are to assist them in their business.

Exercise 5: How Are You Different?

Every firm at its core believes that it is great and has the best solution for clients to implement. What makes you different from your competition? Which three principles make you best in the field? Why do they make your firm different?

Got it?

Great! Write it out! Once you have it on paper, you can continue to refine the areas as you grow.

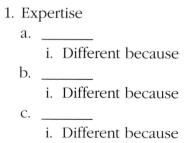

1. Expertise
    a. _____
        i. Different because
    b. _____
        i. Different because
    c. _____
        i. Different because

How Are You Going to Earn Income?

The part of the pitch often the most difficult is the fee schedule. Each person feels (and rightly so) that his or her time is important. As a consultant, putting a proper frame around billable hours can be tricky. We all feel like our time should be valued at one million dollars per hour, but that is not realistic nor feasible for any client to pay. In creating a fair and profitable fee schedule, several factors should be considered. Time, materials, follow-up, development, and profit should be the figures used for calculation of hourly or by the job rate.

Time is equal to the hours used to prepare for the client—from research to actual training time.

Materials equals everything from pens to handout.

Follow-up equals the returns to the client for additional support or retraining.

Profit equals everything that is leftover after the stakeholders have received their share.

Putting these categories into a formula can help to figure out what area you should set as a rate to generate enough earnings to support you and your business.

Exercise 6: The Formula

So how much is your time really worth? How much is your monetary goal for the year? Let's figure it out. Using this formula, you can figure out what your hourly rate should be. The formula will account for working through a calendar year. In a leap year, just add one day to the equation.

Hence, in a normal (non-leap) year, the formula should look like this:

$$\textit{Base Hourly Rate Equation}$$

$$\frac{22(\textit{Days}) \times 12\ (\textit{Months}) \times 8(\textit{Hours in a Day})}{?(\textit{Your desired goal for the year})}$$

This will give your base hourly rate. This base hourly rate does not account for your health/medical benefits, marketing, insurance, and overtime hours. To find a more accurate hourly rate or true hourly rate, multiply your base hourly rate by 2.5%. Do not forget to take your annual goal up by 2.5%. After doing this, you will know how much you need to make to meet your monetary goal for the year.

True Hourly Rate Equation

Base hourly rate × 2.5 (Benefits, Martketing, Overtime Hours) = True Hourly Rate

It is important to realize that not every job you are contracted for is going to help you with your goal for the year. However, the job could pay in other ways. Contacts in the consulting world are priceless. Know how to sell your services or get your foot in the door through a chance meeting. After pleasantries are given, you need to be ready with your pitch.

The life and afterlife of your elevator pitch should also be reviewed (Figure 9.1).

The first step after the initial contact is not just good manners, it is crucial. Think about how many people you came across at your last conference. Then think about how many e-mails you received that said "Great to meet you last week at the _____ conference! I look forward to speaking with you"—a basic e-mail that will receive a basic response. However, what if in this first contact you sent an article? Asked a question or two about a topic from the conference? The receiver of this e-mail will more than likely respond because you have asked them a question. You have asked them for their opinion. This can lead to more correspondence, and your request for a meeting. The first meeting is where you can discuss with the potential client what you remember their issues to be and how you can be of service soon. When the first meeting is established, do not walk into it empty handed.

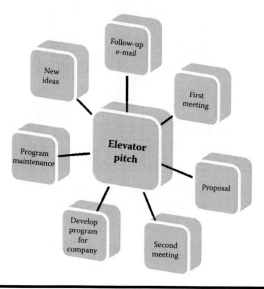

Figure 9.1   The pitch.

Begin preparations for your formal proposal to your new client. This proposal should include a concise message of what services you will provide, how long this training or programming will take, and the cost involved. Tips and assistance for crafting proposals will be discussed later in the chapter.

Since you have crafted your pitch, also review other ways to get your information out to the public.

Self-Promotion

> Self-promotion is a leadership and political skill that is critical to master in order to navigate the realities of the workplace and position you for success.
>
> **Bonnie Marcus**

To further simplify the definition of *self-promotion*, the *Psychology Dictionary* states that it is how we make ourselves look good to others by highlighting our competence and abilities. Let us look at another scenario.

You have written down some of your best crafted ideas on topics related to organization and succession plans. You also want to use these works to advance your efforts in the consulting world.

Where do you begin? What path do you take to get your message out? How do you craft your materials for self-promotion?

Do not think of self-promotion as just a linear science, it is just as much art as it is science. Science is the linear path for getting a successful outcome. Art is the outside-of-the-box thinking that leads to a nontraditional way to generate sales and produce leads. To understand self-promotion, examine the science part first.

The traditional ways of self-promotion include writing articles for journals, magazines, and editorials. Getting your name in print, in well-established trade magazines or journals, can give your level of expertise additional exposure to the market. Although many people consider printed materials a dying medium, it is still the first stop for a great deal of decision makers. Short articles can be sent as an attachment to potential clients. These quick glimpses of your ideas can sway a client from potential client to actual client. Longer articles, typically those found in trade journals such as the Association for Talent Development (www.td.org) and National Association of Colleges and Employers (www.baceweb.org), should be given to a client in person with points highlighted. The recipient can get right to the main points meant for them, and then they review the article at their own pace. However, if you are trying to impress potential clients, give them a signed copy of your book. Just like with the article you presented to them, draw their attention to a chapter or chapters that could help in their current situation. By highlighting solutions to their particular problems, you show two things: first, you have a general understanding of their unique problem, and second, you have a solution vetted and tried and has worked in another similar situation. The client now has basic understanding of what you want to do for them. This information can be taken up to a decision maker, if the materials have not reached them already. The goal for this material is to get it in the hands of someone who can decide in your favor. Giving away a book you might sell can generate more profit in the long run than in the initial purchase.

However, books and articles may not reach all of your potential clients. Be prepared to use other methods to contact the market. In recent years, electronic media has become the way to go for outreach! Developing a website should be your first step in entering the current consultant marketplace. According to SiteBuilderReport, the top six sites for website development are

1. Square Space   www.squarespace.com
2. Weebly   www.weebly.com
3. Edicy   www.edicy.com
4. Yola   www.yola.com
5. WordPress   www.wordpress.com
6. Strikingly   www.strikingly.com

Besides the best websites, the best blogging sites as listed by SaveDelete .com are

1. Blogger   www.blogger.com
2. WordPress   www.wordpress.com
3. Tumblr   www.tumblr.com
4. Medium   www.medium.com
5. LiveJournal   www.livejournal.com
6. Quora   www.quora.com

All these sites listed are free sites that have everything from fancy templates (SquareSpace) to the ability to annotate (Tumblr) others' work for later reading and sharing. Another website that deserves review is Pocket (www.pocket.com). While Pocket does not allow for you to put your writings to the web, it allows for you to mark and save articles to send out to people who have concerns about topics in your area of expertise. LinkedIn and Facebook should be used, but not as your main contact sources. These sites should be supplements to your personal blog and website spaces. On LinkedIn, you should have an updated copy of your vita or an elongated copy of your most up-to-date resume. What should be demonstrated in this document is all of your relevant experience. Since this is a digital form of your work and accomplishments, do not limit yourself on length. Some clients may want to review what you have done in its entirety. Having it online gives them the opportunity to look at your work at their leisure. Another great factor about LinkedIn (paid or free versions) is that the site will let you know who is reviewing your information. This is another way you might follow up with a potential client. On Facebook, have your conference presentations video posted to your pages. Video from conferences only enhance your brand, and you can display the topic when you upload content to either page. Both sites provide excellent opportunities for networking, but for optimum use, link them together. Linking the two sites will allow you to contact possible clients on a broader scale. As these two sites work on establishing you in the consulting world, gaining a following will hopefully not be a problem. It is at this point you should direct people to a Twitter page. The rationale in waiting to have a Twitter account is to ensure that you have a following of people you can send posts. Those people receiving your posts will hopefully find something of value to retweet. People retweeting your posts can expose your ideas and experiences to a whole new group of people. Besides submitting your thoughts to your own electronic spaces, you can also submit articles to various trade sources. Submitting to sites like Slate (www.slate.com), Huffington Post (http://www.huffingtonpost.com), IJReview (http://www.ijreview.com/), and The Weekly Standard (http://www.weeklystandard.com/) could also serve as additional ways to put your name in front of potential clients. These sites are more "news" and information. Do not forget or overlook submitting articles to professional journals such as *HR Professionals* (http://hrprofessionalsmagazine.com), *Workforce* (http://www.workforce.com/), and *HRM America* (http://www.hrmamerica.com). Newspaper editorial pages are also still a viable way to put your name in front of people who will see you as an expert in a chosen field. In reviewing all of the ways to promote your knowledge, be careful! Now is your time to be cautious and selective about what articles you send in for submission, and where you send them. Your name is your commodity; it will only be as strong as your choices for publication. A few quick rules for submissions to journals:

1. In the beginning, attempt to publish in a journal that has a smaller distribution. It would be good to start here so you can become familiar with the submissions process.
2. Peer review journals may be harder to get into and have a smaller readership, but the respect for the quality work in these types of journal can carry your brand a long way.
3. Rejection is not always a bad thing.
   a. Most journals will give feedback on what needs to be improved in your article for acceptance.
4. Consider the validity of the journal. If they ask you to pay before publishing your work, they may not be reputable.
5. Be patient, decisions on your work may not come quickly, reviews take time.

A last note on self-promotion: The US Postal Service can be your ally to grab a share of the marketplace. Believe it or not, direct mailing is still a viable way to reach potential clients. Sending a letter to a potential client still can create a strong presence for you. According to Robert Bly of Peter DeLegge marketing, "A package with a letter will nearly always out pull a postcard, a self-mailer, or a brochure or ad reprint mailed without a letter. ...a letter creates the illusion of personal communication. We are trained to view letters as 'real' mail, brochures as 'advertising.'" If you are wondering what to stay away from in direct mailing, stay away from post cards. Post cards are usually the first thing people dismiss after quick glance. A letter in an envelope will cause clients to take a little more time with your information. People will read something that is addressed to them. Those few, brief extra seconds can be all it takes to generate business for you. The mailing list comes from those persons you have contacted or have given a presentation. In completing your tool box for your promotional items, also have some general presentations ready to be delivered in case you are called upon short notice.

Presentations

According to Dr. Mark Gelula, "adults are typically pragmatic in their learning purposes. They look to achieve specific needs or meet certain interests. Effective lecturers present to those needs and interests."

You are called to present for a midsize company, to talk about your area of expertise. What do you do? How do you construct the presentation? What medium do you use? Are you prepared to handle the size of the audience?

When you develop a presentation, there are several things to take in consideration: the size of the audience, the level of the audience's understanding of the topic, the venue itself, and lastly, are you comfortable with presenting the information requested?

The components of competent presentation is

1. Structure
2. Content
3. Medium
4. Delivery

Structure

If you built a house, you would want it built on a solid foundation. A good presentation is not much different in that regard. Presentations must have structure that will allow your audience to follow with ease. The information being presented is generated by your client. The format is up to you. In the beginning it will be important to ask the client the audience. It will also be important to know of the understanding of the topic that your audience has. Audiences may have a strong frame of reference on your topic so you would not need to go through major concepts in a detailed manner, but if this information is new to your customers, you will need to walk them through each point of the information. The initial structure should demonstrate a respect for the audience. The structured presentation should not be overrun with large verbose vocabulary. Your word section should be accurate and concise; the less syllables in the word structuring of the presentation the better. Another consideration in constructing your presentation should be the size of the audience. There different approaches are necessary for the size of the group. For instance, if your audience is a small group, have them introduce themselves to you as a way to break the ice, which can be helpful if they do not know each other. In larger groups, you cannot get to know any of the group until after the presentation or during a question and answer segment. This means you have to be prepared to have a presentation that will allow you to connect with a group that you may not physically be able to see. In structuring this presentation, understand what message the client wants you to convey. A request for a presentation that trains a group will differ from a presentation on mentoring that is serving as a motivational call to action. Both talks are about mentoring but have two distinct and different directions. Talking to the client gains a clear understanding of your purpose of the presentation and will help you to meet their needs. Knowing the venue will be crucial to your success. The size of room will also determine how you can present your information. In Exercise 7, you can lay out a basic structure of how your presentation should be done.

Exercise 7: Laying the Foundation

When you are contracted to speak, there should be several questions you ask your employer. Here are questions that should be asked to help you deliver an outstanding presentation. Question 4 could be your opening question or the last question. You should make sure you understand how much time is being committed for your information.

1. How many people are you speaking to?
   a. Do they have any information on the topic?
   b. Are they forced to be present?
   c. Is this important to them?
2. What is the point of the presentation?
   a. Informational, motivational, training
3. How is the room configured?
   a. Will there be a stage?
   b. Can I walk around the room?
   c. Are the microphones wired or cordless?
4. How much time do I have?

With a foundation now firmly laid, creation of content is the next step.

Content

Similar to how your structure was developed, your content is created the same way. Imparting knowledge can be a difficult thing. So how your information is put together is a very important contributor to your success. Key elements of your content should include the introduction, the information, an action, and a conclusion.

Introduction

The introduction should establish your creditability. This information can either be given verbally or placed within your presentation. Creditability can be established by stating work experience; it can also be demonstrated by discussing the level of research you have done that relates to the area. The last thing to establish yourself as an expert is the level of education. The audience will assume, usually, that you have obtained the education to be in the front of the room; they want to know what you have done that will help them in their current situation. It should also set up the rest of the presentation and provide a framework that the audience can understand of what is coming next. Consider the introduction to be the road map you want the audience to follow.

Information

The audience now understands your intentions, their attention is completely on you, and they are primed and ready to receive the information you have to give them! The information you are providing is important. Treat it as if it means everything to you. When conveying the information they need, remember your audience. Is this a group that would prefer to be lectured to or is this a group that would benefit from a hands-on demonstration, role playing, and interactive conversations? The content should be crisp and concise. When the audience hears it for the first time, can they see how to make this information work for them in their daily task? As you convey this information to your audience, can they understand why the information provided is important to their success? As you craft this information, put yourself in your audience's chair. If you heard this information, would it relate to you? Does this content represent what your client wanted you to provide to the audience? Once the answers to these questions become clear, you will be better suited to craft information that is not only insightful but also meaningful to your customer (audience) and client. The information can also provide points for the audience to think about. The content can serve as a call to action for the audience.

Exercise 8: Informing the Audience

When you are speaking to large or small groups, they want to know who you are. Deciding what to tell your audience about yourself can give you more creditability. However, before telling everyone just how great you are, take notice of your audience. While most audiences want both, they usually lean to wanting to know more about you personally or academically. See if you can answer the following questions from a personal, then an academic, point of view and a combination of the two.

1. Who are you?
2. What have you done?
3. Should you disclose your educational attainment?
4. Is this presentation about a topic directly related to your firm?
   a. You may be called on to give a presentation that has nothing to do with your firm's expertise.
5. Can the information be understood?
6. What do you want the audience to take away?

Call to Action

At this phase of the presentation, your audience ready to get to work, because there is something they must accomplish. This is where your call to action should tell the audience the next steps, and how the change should begin. The audience should be given a plan that will lead to some desired, tangible result. If your topic was about mentoring in the workplace, those in attendance should believe that they can engage in a mentoring program with the tools they have been given. After hearing the presentation, they should also feel empowered to seek opportunities to use their skills. This call is important because it provides direction to the audience. It allows your information to become a living presentation. The audience can now feel confident in their efforts in the workplace.

Exercise 9: Heeding the Call

The point of every training is to provide good information that can be used or implemented when the talk is over. If you were preparing to give a presentation or training tomorrow, could you concisely answer the following questions?

1. What should the audience be doing after hearing the information?
2. Can the customer practically apply the information given to work situations?
3. How much can the call to action change behavior?

Conclusion

Your conclusion should be a wrap up of all previous ideas discussed during the presentation. Spur-of-the-moment adjustments should be avoided during the conclusion. Only previously discussed information should be talked about during this portion of your message. The conclusion should also restate your name and contact information. It should also allow for the audience to ask questions and possibly engage with you about doing follow up visits.

Medium

Modern technology has given presenters incredible power! Ten years ago, a presentation *might* have been recorded; in 2016, it is hard to think of a presentation that will not be recorded. In fact, YouTube has a considerable amount of videos dedicated to professionals providing their wisdom and ideas to small group of individuals, yet after the recording is over, it the same talk can be viewed by as many as one million people. An example of the successful use of this type of medium for consultants would be Alan Weiss. He records *everything* he does! More importantly, he puts it on the Internet. If he gives a talk, interview, or lecture—it is recorded. He currently has over 200 videos ranging from 35 seconds to 120 minutes. He is a good example of how to use digital media to get your message out. In the near future, review his channel on YouTube to get a better idea about self-promotion through digital media. Another medium that is tried and true are books. When working with a multigenerational organization, just having an online presence may not be enough. Some of the team may want to have a tangible item that details your thought process in a given area, not just a planned speech. Written materials also give you the ability to "stay" with your client when they are not in the office or online. Remember, giving a prospective client one of your works on the subject they are considering hiring you for can be advantage over a competitor. Offering your written work to a prospective client does one other important thing, it keeps your name in front of the client. Using a book or an article that you have written is the oldest form direct marketing, but it still works!

Delivery

This is the best part of the presentation. It's the best part for one reason, and one reason alone. That reason is YOU. You have given presentations before; you already know what strengths and weaknesses you have when it comes to public speaking. However, it is just as important to realize every visual cue is important, just as every auditory cue is equally important. When preparing to give a pitch or speech, you should try to know the following:

1. The culture of the group.
   a. Do they respond better to call and response or do they just want to be lectured?
   b. Are they qualitative (want stories) or quantitative (just facts and numbers) listeners?
   c. Would they voice their ideas without prompting?
2. What time in the workday are speaking with the team.
   a. Before or after lunch: was the team requested to attend over their lunch break?
   b. Are you speaking right before closing?
   c. Did the group have to come in early to attend your presentation?
3. (When possible) How is the room configured?
   a. Is the room hot or cold?
   b. What is the lighting like in the room?
   c. Can you walk around, or do you have to stay in one place?

The client can give you a wealth of information on the environment that you are speaking in, but knowing the little details will help you have an outstanding presentation. You may also want to visit the site (if you can) for a quick walk through. If you need to practice, and you cannot use the area, getting a picture in your mind of the room can be very helpful. Your delivery is about mainly your style. Keep the basic rules of public speaking in front of you: make eye contact, be mindful of your time, respect your audience, allow the audience to be an active listener, be honest and sincere, and lastly but most importantly, smile. A smile is sometimes your only defense to win over a tough crowd.

So as the quote goes "To thine own self be true"—remember this in your delivery. Being true to your speaking style is best way to have an effective delivery when giving a presentation.

Proposal Writing

For an independent OD consultant, there is no sitting back and letting business fall into your lap. OD consultants must always look for new avenues of revenue. Competing for government contracts is an excellent way to accomplish this.

You are attending a conference, after hearing your elevator pitch and seeing your presentation, a company official requests that you submit a proposal for work.

Do you understand what the proposal should have in it? Are you familiar with components of a successful grant proposal? Should you take on multiple proposals?

A *proposal* allows you to seek funding from an outside entity or group to start, give support to, or maintain a program. To have a successful proposal, you need to describe precisely your immediate purposes (or hypotheses or research questions) and sketch the long-term goal or potential usefulness of the research (Tornquist & Funk, 1990). The proposal should open with a general overview. The reading should be interesting so the grant reviewer will want to continue to read and see how the experiments/ research is resolved. After the overview, the question must be expressed. Remember, you want to keep the hypotheses simple. It will be important to identify the setting in which the grant will be implemented. This will be accompanied by explaining what type of sample size you will work with. There will need to be a definite plan action from methods to budget. To get things started, here are the basic elements of a proposal: cover letter, title page, table of contents, summary, qualifications of the organization, statement of problem, objectives and goals, methods, evaluation, and budget.

A good resource for developing grant writing skills is Grant Space (www .grantspace.org). The Foundation Center (http://foundationcenter.org/getstarted /tutorials/shortcourse/) also provides excellent advice on proposal preparation. In 2005, Kent State University's Division of Research and Graduate Studies (2005) supplied a great outline for writing proposals. In planning and writing proposals, this is a good guide to follow.

The Proposal Steps

1. Title Page
2. Abstract
3. Table of Contents with List of Tables and/or Illustrations
4. Project Description
    a. Introduction
    b. Problem Statement
    c. Objectives
    d. Methodology
    e. Personnel
    f. Facilities
    g. Evaluation Plan
5. Budget
6. List of References
7. Bibliography
8. Appendices

While you may not receive a positive outcome for every proposal you submit a document for, this format should help to make sure you have a strong and complete proposal to present.

Client Management

Your current client is concerned that you are becoming too popular in the OD market and is demanding more of your time. This client has never been a high-touch client before but seems to have many issues now.

How do you handle this situation?

Once a contract is signed, that is when the real work begins. Client management can be a very challenging situation. In your start-up phase, you may have time to deal directly with all of your clients. As you grow, that may not be the case. You must allow your business to grow, but you can never do it to the client, no matter the revenue they generate. If you treat every client like it is a million dollar account, you can never go wrong. This is a difficult thing to do. As an OD consultant, you are contracted to help turn a company around; some clients become reliant on your good judgment. This means they will expect you to be there at the first sign of trouble and call, despite your having other appointment with clients. This scenario is typical for most consultants. Being prepared to handle perceived problems starts right after you being to provide services. Follow-up with current clients is a must. Conduct in-person visits to see if the programs you put in place are being followed before you receive the call telling you something is wrong. Call to see if there is anything else that is needed or to discuss ideas for additional programming to supplement the work you have already done. The client should be introduced (if possible) to every member of your team who may interact with them regularly. You should never spring a new person on a client. Each introduction should be done so the clients understand that they are valued. Since you secured the business, cultivate it at every turn. When prepared to turn the client over to an associate, you must be there for the transition and introduction. This way, the client knows that the person you have sent comes with your personal blessing and is not just some random employee who does not understand this client's business. When you have successfully made this transition, you can then move on to new business. However, even though your presence will be less, you still must make time to interact with the client. Whether you host the client for lunch or a round of golf or work together on a community service project, keeping the relationship strong will keep the business thriving and the problems down.

Client management can really be considered as relationship management. If you treat your client relationship as a relationship you have to actively work at, you have a strong possibility of succeeding.

Over the course of this chapter, we have worked on various ways for you to stake your claim in the crowded field of consultants! You have now defined what an OD consultant does. Your elevator pitch has now been honed to be a concise, impactful statement of information that will not only get you in the door but also create an opportunity for recurring business. You are prepared to write grants and proposals to secure business when things are slow. The management of clients and management of relationships are almost the same to you. The subsequent chapters will further help you with your communication and negotiation skills.

References

Hayden, C. (2013). Get clients now! A 28-day marketing program for professionals, consultants, and coaches (3rd ed.). New York: American Management Association.

Kent State University. (2005). Proposal preparation guide. *Methodology*. Retrieved from http://www.kent.edu/research/sponsoredprograms/upload/Proposal _Preparation_Guide.pdf

MacLean, R. (2012). The elevator pitch. *Environmental Quality Management, 21,* 99–105. doi:10.1002/tqem.21312

Rothwell, W. J., & Sredl, H. J. (2000). *The ASTD reference guide to workplace learning and performance: Present and future roles and competencies* (3rd ed.). Amherst, MA: HRD Press.

Tornquist, E. M., & Funk, S. G. (1990). How to write a research grant proposal. *Image: the Journal of Nursing Scholarship, 22*(1), 44–51.

Weiss, A. (2009). *Million dollar consulting: The professional's guide to growing a practice* (4th ed.). New York: McGraw-Hill.

Chapter 10

Executive-Level Communications

Jae Young Lee

Contents

Differences Between Internal and External OD Consultants 161
Business Case Studies 161
   How Would You Approach C-Level Executives to Market Your Service? 161
      Case 1 161
      Case 2 162
      Case 3 162
      Case 4 163
      Case Discussion 163
Methods of Accessing C-Level Executives 163
   Climb Up the Authorized Ladder 163
   Build Networks with Linchpins Within the Organization 165
   Improve Credibility and Visibility 166
Tips for Executive-Level Communications 168
   Help Them to Understand the Difference Between OD Consulting
   and Management Consulting 169
   Remind Them That OD Is Their Responsibility 169
   Focus on What C-Level Executives Are Interested In 170

Persuade Them on Even Ground 170
Make Opportunities for Continuous Communication 171
Keep Your Communication Simple 171
Summary 172
References 172

Ways for organization development (OD) consultants to penetrate all barriers to get to C-level executives, as well as useful tips for communicating with these executives throughout consulting projects are provided in this chapter. Meetings and consensus-building with C-level executives are critical for OD consultants because senior executives shape values and lead changes within the organization. They not only control an organization's resources and systems but also serve as role models for people in the organization. In this regard, communication with C-level executives is important since "OD works best when it is supported by top managers" (Rothwell, Stravros, Sullivan, R.L. & Sullivan A., 2010, p. 14).

Accessing C-level executives is difficult in any organization. Although you might have excellent ideas for changing the organization, and you might also provide outstanding services as an OD consultant, politics and the layers of gatekeepers may serve to bar you from the executives' door. If you are an internal OD consultant, you must work through the bureaucracy in the organization to reach the C-level executives. If you are an external OD consultant, you may have little information about the key person in an organization who can take you to executives.

Even if you pass most hurdles to gain access to the executives, one still remains between you and the executives. Often, C-level executives know little about OD. Even if they know what OD is, they are usually not familiar with OD consultants' approaches to making organizational changes. OD consultants do not dictate change but let people in the organization determine next steps and actions. Executives may not understand why OD consultants do not provide direct and quick solutions in the same manner as other management consultants do. If you are an external OD consultant, once the executives understand your role, they may think that their people can do better than you. If you are an internal OD consultant, they may question your professionalism and may not recognize your capacity to make changes. Being an insider is the issue here. Therefore, OD consultants should know how to communicate with C-level executives about OD and persuade them that they need OD consultants. Once OD consultants persuade executives, the consultants should extract promises of full support from them.

In the rest of this chapter, we review the differences between internal and external OD consultants in order to identify the proper strategies for obtaining access to C-level executives. Then several suggestions are offered for communicating and persuading executives.

Differences Between Internal and External OD Consultants

OD consultants are either internal or external consultants to organizations. Internal OD consultants are members of and work for their organizations full time. External OD consultants generally work for consulting firms or themselves and are hired by clients for a certain period. If an OD department works for a chief executive officer (CEO) directly, the department and the CED usually have a close relationship and frequent communication. However, if the OD function is in the human resource (HR) department, internal OD consultants' role is usually vague and they have difficulty gaining access to the C-level executives due to the multiplicity of leadership layers to navigate.

Both internal and external consultants have their own advantages and disadvantages. Internal consultants are members of organizations, so they know their organizations' people, culture, language, policy, politics, and business in depth. This knowledge usually gives internal consultants unique insights when identifying the "root cause(s)" of an organization's problem. These intuitive perceptions result in time savings for consultants at the beginning of an OD project compared to external consultants. However, internal consultants are not free from their organizations' power structures and political issues. In this respect, external consultants have advantages, such as being unbiased and neutral when dealing with problems. Table 10.1 shows the advantages and disadvantages of internal and external OD consultants.

Business Case Studies

How Would You Approach C-Level Executives to Market Your Service?

Case 1

After getting a master's degree in OD, you have started your own consulting business as an OD consultant. You have seven years of experience at a local

Table 10.1   Advantages and Disadvantages of Internal and External OD Consultants

	Internal OD Consultants	*External OD Consultants*
Advantages	• Understand company's jargon, politics, and culture • In-depth knowledge of the business, organization history, norms, informal practices, and work processes • Strong networks within the organization • Accessibility to a variety of information • Secure company's confidentiality • Insight into the *root causes*	• Viewed as having higher expertise than internal consultants • Higher status than employees • Free from politics and unbiased toward other organizational factors • Retain objectivity • Able to select projects according to their criteria
Disadvantages	• Little recognition • Biased and easily affected by politics and leadership • Must work through power structure and bureaucracy • Not allowed to select projects	• Time-consuming process to build relationships within organizations and learn their cultures • Sometimes called in because nobody wanted to get his or her hands dirty

manufacturing company as an HR manager, so you think you are specialized in succession planning.

Case 2

Your company is a global insurance company, and you have been working there for 12 years as an OD consultant. Recently, your company has experienced a high turnover rate, especially among entry-level employees. You heard from your close colleague in the HR department that C-level executives are concerned about this high turnover and its ramifications for to the organization.

Case 3

After working as an OD consultant at a consulting firm for a decade, you were scouted as a senior OD department manager by one of your client companies. You know that the company hired you because they wanted overall changes within the organization, but nobody tells you exactly what to do.

Case 4

Near the end of your short-term teambuilding project for your client company, you think it will be more effective for the company to successively provide coaching programs to its senior-level managers. You want to suggest your executive coaching program to your client.

Case Discussion

1. In each case, identify the OD consultant's status.
2. In each case, identify the advantages and disadvantages of the given status.
3. How can the consultant gain access to C-level executives?
4. How can the consultant market him- or herself and the available services to C-level executives?

Methods of Accessing C-Level Executives

C-level executives are consistently short on time and usually protected by gatekeepers, so it is not easy even for internal high-level managers to meet with them. For this reason, it is almost impossible for external consultants to reach C-level executives directly by phone or e-mail. Despite these unfavorable conditions, OD consultants should meet with C-level executives because they possess the power and authority to approve and support their projects. There are direct and indirect ways to reach C-level executives; this chapter will reveal three commonly used access methods:

■ Climb up the authorized ladder
■ Build networks with linchpins within the organization
■ Improve credibility and visibility

Climb Up the Authorized Ladder

This is the most typical manner through which internal OD consultants gain access to executives; however, the chance of success is low. Even though you may have a great idea for changing your organization, your boss or your boss's boss may not agree with you. Getting through all these layers of leadership takes time and is sometimes frustrating. Worse yet, sometimes the process is blocked at some level and does not move further. However, a few people succeed in climbing up this ladder and achieving their goals. Usually, they are veterans who have earned the organization's trust via outstanding performance. They also have the ability to monitor and follow the organization's urgent issues. Building this credibility and visibility takes time. What if you do not have enough experience to build up your own reputation? One answer is to demonstrate good communication skills in order to persuade your boss.

As an internal OD consultant, the successful climb up the authorized ladder to the top requires that you first persuade your boss. Green (2013) suggested several effective methods:

- Make your plan specific so that it is easy for your boss to say "yes."
- Identity the right timing by considering the company's atmosphere.
- Focus on the advantages for the company.
- Demonstrate that you have already thought out the pros and cons.
- Preemptively suggest alternatives; if your boss seems hesitant, ask for a pilot test.
- If your boss says "no," identify and provide the information that might change his or her mind.

Keep in mind that simple and easy messages work better. Do not allow your bosses to think or interpret your message in their own way. The right timing is also very important. No managers want to approve new training programs when their CEO is highly sensitive to the worst performance of the year. To get your boss's approval, your argument should be persuasive. This requires the consideration of both advantages and disadvantages and the preparation of a list of solutions in advance. If your boss still seems unsure about your plan or focuses on its negative aspects, ask for an experiment. If you fail to gain consent, find out the reasons and see if there is a way to sway the decision back toward your idea.

If an external OD consultant has not been directly brought into the organization by senior management, he or she should both work with lower-level employees and make efforts to reach executives. Lower-level employees are relatively easy to access, and many mid-level managers are aware of the precise nature of their organization's problems (e.g., turnover, teamwork, and succession planning). The OD consultant can identify several problems through meetings with lower-level employees or mid-level managers. During these meetings, the OD consultant and managers can create and narrow down a list of several topics of interest to the executive level. Entry into the organization requires an appeal to the organization's managers about your ability to help resolve problems as well as marketing.

In order to reach the senior executives with the power to approve the OD project, the OD consultant should persuade different levels of people as he or she moves through the organization. As the external OD consultant works with lower-level employees, he or she must provide detailed information about services provided, such as project scope, period, or price. As the consultant climbs up the ladder, these details become less important. Finally, when the consultant has reached the top, he or she should focus on articulating the values of his or her work and the benefits of obtaining those results.

Build Networks with Linchpins Within the Organization

To gain access to C-level executives, OD consultants may take circuitous approaches. Rather than trying to contact the executives, OD consultants can increase OD awareness by speaking with those who surround C-level executives and encouraging them to talk about interventions. If the linchpins think that the OD consultant is valuable, they will recommend the consultant to executives if an OD issue arises. This is called viral marketing, which "use[s] pre-existing social networking services and other technologies to try to produce increases in brand awareness or to achieve other marketing objectives (such as product sales) through self-replicating viral processes" (Wikipedia, 2016, para 1). Viral marketing is a powerful method that works for OD marketing, too.

Rather than trying to meet C-level executives directly, OD consultants should actively contact those close to these executives. Building network allies among their gatekeepers helps OD consultants in several ways. First, OD consultants can gather vital information from the linchpins, including intelligence on recent business issues, C-level executives' worries, and other critical problems within the organization. Access to this information makes a huge difference when selling your service, including increasing your credibility when suggesting a proposal to resolve organization problems that resonates with C-level executives. Through these relationships, external OD consultants can become familiar with their business and organization cultures. Therefore, once they are called in, they can make a good impression on C-level executives by demonstrating that they are knowledgeable about the business and culture of the given organizations.

Second, the linchpins are those who control the information provided to the executives, so OD consultants should work to convince them that OD can add value to the organization. If the key people believe that your ideas have value to the organization, they will recommend you to the executives when they need an OD expert. If you are an internal OD consultant, take advantage of your status. Keeping in mind the key issues obtained from the linchpins, you can gather further information from people in the organization via informal interviews, informal meetings, and simple surveys. Once your research is complete, you can suggest a proposal to key people that includes your services and the probable impacts of your work on the organization.

The cultivation of this relationship ensures access to C-level executives and aids both external and internal consultants. Since these people are the key influences on both C-level executives and others in the organization, they will be your best supporters and will troubleshoot any difficult situations.

Improve Credibility and Visibility

According to Weiss (2009), the best way to marketing yourself is to create a 'gravity' that draws people to you. The presence of gravity changes the dynamics between sellers and consumers by heightening consumers' interest in the sellers rather than convincing the customers. This phenomenon shows why reputation and word-of-mouth are important. As an OD consultant, in order to draw people to you, you should build credibility and improve visibility.

Internal OD consultants build credibility within their organizations via excellent performance. A series of successes will raise your profile and cause managers to request your involvement in important projects. Building reputation through outstanding performance and gaining the endorsement of your managers will push you up to the top of the authorized ladder.

External OD consultants should also retain favorable publicity. Word spreads quickly, and bad rumors fly. Making a mistake, such as manipulating data, violating confidentiality, or leaking information to a third party, can seriously endanger your career. Increase trust by demonstrating your high level of competency and rigorous ethical standards. If your project was successfully completed, ask your client whether he or she would write a testimonial for your website or brochure. Many will help you if your service met their expectations. They may also agree to act as references for potential clients who may be interested in your services and wish to hear about successful project experiences and outcomes. You can ask your clients to refer you to their colleagues or acquaintances at other companies.

Improving visibility demands spontaneous extra work in addition to the completion of projects. Internal and external OD consultants can improve their visibility by writing articles or books, conducting interviews with the media, blogging or running their own websites, making public speeches, sending newsletters, or networking with other professionals. Internal OD consultants may find that writing a book or an article for a magazine or newspaper is a good way to increase their authority at an organization. These consultants are underestimated compared to external consultants; however, publications and third-party reviews of publications help a writer to be recognized as an expert in a field. Recognized as a professional, your boss will listen to you. If your boss likes your idea, he or she will persuade his or her boss, and it will become easier to get close to executives. Another strategy is to send your books or articles to executives and the people around them. Even though they may not read them, they will keep an eye on you and remember your specialty. And when your skills are needed, they will call you in. The publication strategy works for external consultants as well. When organizations have communications or leadership problems, managers, including executives, look for an expert. One well-used strategy when seeking experts is to identify and search for keywords or book titles on the Internet and then check out the authors and their biographies. Publications with your name on them increase your visibility and your chances of obtaining executive buy-in.

When called, consultants should respond to interview requests from the media (e.g., newspapers, radio, or TV). Media exposure can lead to referrals—one never knows who may have watched, read, or listened to a story involving you. Use these opportunities strategically to increase your name recognition. If you do not receive media requests, create your own opportunities by looking for public speaking engagements at in-house training programs, universities, or conferences. After your presentation, be sure your contact information is on your handouts and slides so that people can contact you or refer you to others easily. These public speaking opportunities will skyrocket your visibility.

Use the worksheet in Table 10.2 to begin thinking about what you have done to increase your visibility and what you still need to do. Add more options if necessary and choose doable things from among the options. Write down specific plans for the doable things. You cannot do everything at the same time and you may not be able to do all of the things. Start from your comfort zone and move on to other options.

Table 10.2 A Worksheet to Improve Your Visibility

Improve Visibility			
Directions: Use this worksheet to help you to improve your visibility as an OD consultant. Read each option in the left column and check whether you have attempted this and whether it is doable for you. When you finish, plan your doable options specifically using 5W1H. Add paper or list more options.			
Options	*Have you tried it before?* *Yes No*	*Is this doable?* *Yes No*	*Plan (5W1H)*
Book Publication	☐ ☐	☐ ☐	
Article Publication	☐ ☐	☐ ☐	
Presentation	☐ ☐	☐ ☐	
Teaching	☐ ☐	☐ ☐	
Blog	☐ ☐	☐ ☐	
Newsletter	☐ ☐	☐ ☐	
Media interview	☐ ☐	☐ ☐	
Networking	☐ ☐	☐ ☐	
Etc. ( )	☐ ☐	☐ ☐	

Tips for Executive-Level Communications

After navigating the layers of gatekeepers, you meet with an executive. Making a good impression and building trust with the final decision-maker are essential to winning business and getting support throughout the project. OD consultants may wish to use these tips in communicating with C-level executives in order to convince them to finally sign a contract or provide them with other support.

- Help them to understand the difference between OD consulting and management consulting.
- Remind them that OD is their responsibility.
- Persuade C-level executives on even ground.
- Make opportunities for continuous communication.
- Keep your communication simple.

Help Them to Understand the Difference Between OD Consulting and Management Consulting

Most senior managers are not familiar with OD. Some are familiar with OD's other names such as team-building, coaching, or change management, but they may be confused about OD and its other names. Moreover, they may not understand the OD consultant's approach, which is not to provide them with answers but to facilitate the organization's work to identify solutions to problems. As mentioned in Chapter 1, an OD consultant is not a management consultant. OD consultants help people in the organization to find the root causes of their problems and facilitate the development and implementation of solutions. To aid them in understanding this important difference, OD consultants can send e-mails to C-level executives with attachments containing one- to two-page white papers on OD prior to their initial meeting. When it is not possible to send the information before the meeting, OD consultants should clarify differences at the beginning of their first face-to-face meetings. Since confusion about the OD concept may continue throughout the meeting, it may be necessary for OD consultants to remind them from time to time throughout the project. Often, OD consultants are told that if they are not providing solutions to problems, their role and purpose seem unnecessary. Be prepared for that question before you meet the executives, focusing on the kinds of value you can add to their business, unlike that offered in management consulting, for example.

Remind Them That OD Is Their Responsibility

OD is one of C-level executives' responsibilities. Harvard Business School professor Groysberg (2014) found that one of the most prized executive skills today is change management. Change management is similar to OD. Change management and OD are not the same, but both are related to changing people in an organization. Even though OD is often underappreciated and overlooked by top senior executives due to other urgent business issues, it is one of their important responsibilities. And even if C-level executives know the importance of OD, they usually do not have enough time to consider it when coping with pending business. When conversing with C-level executives, remind them of their OD responsibility and elicit their needs for help from you.

Focus on What C-Level Executives Are Interested In

Executives are decision-makers who make important decisions that add value to their organizations. Executives are not financial managers or contract administrators. They are not interested in cost or details, but they do care about outcomes and business impacts. Explain to them what kind of value you can add to their business and show them how your work may influence the big picture. If they brought you in because of a certain problem, provide the specific request directly and quickly at the beginning of your meeting. Tailor your message to their interest and get down to the nitty-gritty. On the other hand, if you reached out to them, try to listen rather than talk. The more they speak, the more you will know about their needs. If they say nothing, you will lose a chance to learn from your client. Ask them provocative questions and let them speak about their consulting needs.

Usually, C-level executives want to know about what their people think and what their competitors are doing. Since C-level executives are protected by layers of gatekeepers, their information could be unexpectedly limited by public sentiment at the organization. In order to finally meet the executives, you will likely meet many others in the organization and gather much information through formal or informal interviews and surveys. Provide executives with the information that you gathered on how people think about certain problems in the organization. It is also good to know something about how competitors are handling the same problem. If you are an internal consultant, you can gather competitors' information by using your networks or doing research. If you are an external consultant, you have many resources from your own experiences. Tell them other companies' cases within ethical boundaries and arouse interest and needs for change from C-level executives.

Persuade Them on Even Ground

Executives in high positions in organizations may be viewed with fear and concern. However, employees should remember that executives are employees, too. Many C-level executives have typical problems with managing people, organization, and changes. As an OD consultant, you are there to help them, so be confident and on an equal footing with them. Establish a positive relationship and share your experience in OD. Let them know that you have given as much thought to the organization's problems as they have and that your ideas and knowledge have value in resolving these problems. Your confident manner will lead C-level executives to trust you and lead in the long term to a successful project.

Make Opportunities for Continuous Communication

Since it may take time and be difficult to gain access to C-level executives, OD consultants should work to ensure continuous communication with them for several reasons. Throughout a project, continuous communication with C-level executives is crucial. OD is an organization-wide and relatively long-range change. Therefore, without C-level executives' support, OD change efforts may not be successful. The C-level executives are "traditionally the chief power brokers and change agents in any organization" (Rothwell et al., 2010, p. 14). Therefore, OD consultants need continuous communication with C-level executives. In the early phase of a project, OD consultants need to meet C-level executives to reach an agreement on goals and objectives for the project. During the project, OD consultants should constantly communicate with C-level executives to report progress, review critical issues, or resolve conflicts. In the separation phase, OD consultants should report on project results and suggest other possible projects.

One tip to ensure continuous communication with C-level executives is to be concise. When your conversation is going well, time will fly; however, do not stay or spend more time than necessary. Set the meeting time and leave the room on the dot. Do not forget to ask for a follow-up meeting and put your appointment on the executive's calendar before you leave the room.

Keep Your Communication Simple

To communicate effectively, you need to know your audience. C-level executives are time-pressed people and have many things to remember. Provide clear and simple messages rather than a long speech. Lincoln's Gettysburg Address was only about two minutes and had 286 words. Distill your complex idea into a simple and memorable one.

Avoid a detailed proposal or report (James, 2009). A well-organized and fully researched one-page paper is better than 100 detailed pages. However, this does not mean you should prepare only a one-page document when meeting with executives. While you may hand them one page, you should have backup data and related, detailed information when it's needed. Once executives are interested in something, they may drill down into one of the issues in your paper. You should be ready to respond to their questions, objections, or concerns. Since they are at the peak of their careers and at the top of the organization, they know the company's business better than anyone and are constantly concerned about their business. In order to meet their expectations, you should have information beyond that provided in a one-page report.

Summary

We have discussed how internal and external consultants may access C-level executives and communicate with them. Communication with C-level executives is vital to OD consulting because these executives have the authority to initiate changes in organizations. The next chapter offers a discussion of the evaluation methods that may be used to prove the value of your OD services and the communication skills that should be used in reporting evaluation results.

References

Green, A. (2013). 8 ways to persuade your boss to say yes. Retrieved from http://money.usnews.com/money/blogs/outside-voices-careers/2013/11/06/8-ways-to-persuade-your-boss-to-say-yes

Groysberg, B. (March 2014). The seven skills you need to thrive in the C-suite. *Harvard Business Review.* Retrieved from https://hbr.org/2014/03/the-seven-skills-you-need-to-thrive-in-the-c-suite/

James, G. (June 18, 2009). How to sell to a C-level executive. Retrieved from http://www.cbsnews.com/news/how-to-sell-to-a-c-level-executive/

Rothwell, W. J., Stravros, J. M., Sullivan, R. L., & Sullivan, A. (Eds.). (2010). *Practicing organization development: A guide for leading change* (3rd ed.). San Francisco: Pfeiffer.

Weiss, A. (2009). *Million dollar consulting: The professional's guide to growing a practice* (4th ed.). McGraw-Hill.

Wikipedia (2016). Retrieved from https://en.wikipedia.org/wiki/Viral_marketing

Chapter 11

How Measurement and Appraisal Can Be the Means to the End of Marketing OD

Patricia Macko

Contents

Purpose of Chapter 174
Marketing OD Business Case Scenario 174
A Historical Perspective of Moving from Evaluation to Appraisal 176
Aspects of the Marketing Mix to Consider as a Marketing OD Consultant.... 177
Defining Measurement and Appraisal 181
Importance of Marketing OD Measurement and Appraisal 182
How to Complete Measurement and Appraisal 183
ROI Methodology 185
Why Do Marketing OD Interventions Fail? 186
Summary 186
References 187

Purpose of Chapter

This chapter provides a high-level overview of the relevance of measurement and appraisal in marketing organization development (OD). Several topics of review will be the following:

- Marketing OD business case scenario
- Historical perspective of measurement and evaluation
- Aspects of the marketing mix to consider as a marketing OD consultant
- Defining marketing OD measurement and appraisal (appraisal vs. evaluation)
- Importance of completing marketing measurement and appraisal
- How to measure and appraise marketing OD interventions
- Importance of calculating return on investment (ROI)
- Failures in marketing OD measurement
- Summary

Marketing OD Business Case Scenario

Marti Smith has just received a call from Emergent Credit Union. Marti is a marketing OD consultant with 22 years of experience. Twelve of these years were spent working with the financial services industry. Emergent is one of the largest credit unions in the state of Georgia. Over the past five years, Emergent opened three new branches and hired 25 new employees. Although Emergent appears to be growing, the organization is experiencing slow growth in new customer acquisition in the areas surrounding new branches, struggling to retain current customers, and is experiencing increasing overall expense levels. Emergent has a new vice president of marketing who has convinced the chief executive officer of Emergent that it is time to hire an outside marketing OD consultant to assist the organization with current struggles. Marti can't wait to get started and help Emergent identify and implement a successful marketing OD intervention. Among the many areas that Marti will investigate with Emergent, one of the important areas she must understand is how the organization measures and appraises the overall success of their marketing efforts. Marti also realizes that as a marketing OD consultant, she must understand the area of measurement and appraisal of the overall intervention and the value it will bring to the organization's bottom-line.

Discussion questions that automatically come to mind for Marti are the following.

1. What does Emergent's current strategic marketing plan include?
2. Who is involved with setting the strategic marketing objectives for the organization?
3. What are the capabilities and experience of the employees handling the strategic marketing plan?
4. Who is responsible for the overall monitoring, tracking, completion, and success of the marketing efforts and plan?
5. How will the organization measure and appraise the overall performance of Marti as the external consultant?

Over the next six months Marti works with Emergent to identify a marketing intervention that she and the organization agree will help overcome several of the challenges, such as new customer acquisition, customer retention, and expense reduction. Before implementing the intervention, Marti knows the importance of monitoring, tracking, and assessing how the implementation is going each step of the way. She and the organization must gauge several areas. Several questions Marti will ponder are as follows.

1. Who will lead the project?
2. Who will develop an overall communication plan to employees regarding this marketing intervention?
3. How will the communication plan be distributed to employees?
4. What metrics must be evaluated during implementation and after implementation to measure and appraise success?
5. How will these measurements and appraisal be shared with key stakeholders?
6. What systems or tools will be used to measure and appraise?
7. Who will be responsible for the measurement and appraisal?

The implementation phase lasts for three months, and Marti believes that things have gone pretty smoothly. Marti also knows that the intervention isn't complete yet. She knows that she must now go back and review her initial contract that spells out how the overall success of the marketing intervention will be measured and appraised. The agreement lists the following aspects of measurement and appraisal.

1. When will the measurement and appraisal begin after implementation is complete?
2. Who and how will the communication regarding the findings be shared to all stakeholders?
3. What are the metrics that were designed to measure and appraise?
4. What affect is the intervention having on the 8 P's of the organization? (Product, place, price, promotion, people, processes, performance, and philosophy)
5. How does Emergent rate Marti on her overall marketing consultant performance?

A Historical Perspective of Moving from Evaluation to Appraisal

The most widely known and used model of measurement and evaluation is presented in Kirkpatrick's Four Levels of Evaluation Model (Kirkpatrick, & Kirkpatrick, 2006). His basic premise of considering evaluation was to consider steps that include measuring reaction, learning, behavior, and results. In the 1970s, Jack Phillips added a fifth step of determining ROI with a 10-step process (Phillips, 2011). Phillip's V-Model is a method used to ensure business alignment. The V-Model uses five levels of evaluation, including the following:

Level 1: Reaction to the intervention
Level 2: Learning: skills and knowledge
Level 3: Behavior Change: application of skills and knowledge use
Level 4: Impact measures linked to the intervention
Level 5: ROI: comparison on monetary benefits to the total cost of the intervention

The addition of Level 5 was instrumental to developing how marketing OD intervention is shaped today. As budgets are being squeezed, organizations must be able to measure and appraise the overall success of all marketing OD efforts.

Notice that in this chapter, the term *appraise* has been added to replace the term *evaluation*. Over the years, practitioners and consultants have challenged the difference between the terms evaluate and appraise. The term *evaluation* relates to reviewing how well the intervention was implemented or measured. The word *appraise* not only encompasses how well the intervention was implemented and measured but also takes into consideration the overall value the implemented intervention brings to the organization.

Aspects of the Marketing Mix to Consider as a Marketing OD Consultant

With any marketing initiative, the marketing OD consultant must understand the organization marketing mix. For years, the marketing mix included the four P's of marketing. These four P's include the organization's product, place, price, and promotion. However, as a marketing OD consultant, one must understand a modern approach to the marketing mix. This modern approach includes an additional four P's. These P's include the organization's people, processes, performance, and philosophy. Each one of the 8 P's must be reviewed and understood by the marketing OD consultant in order to assist an organization with deciding which marketing OD intervention is needed.

In reviewing the additional 4 P's consisting of people, processes, performance, and philosophy, the marketing OD consultant is considering the following:

1. People: this consists of areas such as the employee expertise, capabilities, functional area relationships, relationships with customers, leadership development, and attitudes.
2. Processes: this consists of areas such as how the organization handles total quality management, customer relationship management, product research and development, marketing strategies and plan development, project management, and innovation.
3. Performance: this consists of areas such as how the organization measures and appraises productivity, profitability, sales or revenue growth, expense reduction efforts, marketing plan adherence and completion, and innovation.
4. Philosophy: this consists of areas such as the mission, vision, and core values of the organization; strategic planning; global awareness; community involvement; and succession planning.

As a marketing OD consultant, it is critically important to understand the client's overall marketing plan so that you can assist the organization with identifying areas of the plan to improve or enhance. There are many ways for marketing OD consultants to review current plans. Developing an outline or checklist such as the one in Table 11.1 is helpful.

Table 11.1 Marketing OD Consultant Marketing Plan Checklist

External market environment	• What does the economic environment look like? • What does the technological environment look like? • What does the political environment look like? • What does the cultural and social environment look like?
Customer analysis	• How does the organization identify and segment its markets? • What are the customer's key psychological and social influences on buying? • What are the relationships with the customers? • What are the demographics of the customers?
Competitor analysis	• Who are the current competitors of the market? • Who are the emerging competitors of the market? • How does the organization compete with the current competitors? • What are the current barriers to competing? • What is the organization's competitive advantage that helps them compete?
Company analysis	• What does the company's most current SWOT analysis reveal? (Organization's strengths, weaknesses, opportunities, and threats) • What are the organization's overall resources to pull from? (Employees, subcontractors, partners, stakeholders) • What are the overall financial objectives? (Short-term, 1–2 years; long-term, 3–5 years) • What are the overall marketing objectives?
Marketing information requirements	• What are the organizations marketing research needs (with respect to customers, competitors, marketing mix, research, and development)? • What are the organization's secondary and primary data needs? • What are the organizations marketing information systems needs? (Customer information management systems, marketing models)

(Continued)

Table 11.1 (Continued) Marketing OD Consultant Marketing Plan Checklist

Product or services	• What is the product or service class? (Type of consumer or business product) • What is the product or service life cycle? • What stages are the products or services in within the life cycle? • What are the specifications of current products or services? (Features, quality) • What is the branding of the product or service? • What packaging is done with product or services? (Reference to bundling of services) • What cultural sensitivity may exist to product or service?
Place	• Where are the current facilities? (Retailers, wholesalers, warehousing, and distribution) • What are the current channels of distribution? (Direct, indirect) • What degree of market exposure is needed? • What does the facilities plan look like for short-term (1–2 years) and long-term (3–5) years? • How will marketing functions be shared throughout the channels of distribution?
Promotion	• What are the major message themes for the integrated marketing communications (positioning in the market)? • What is the promotion blend? (Advertising, personal selling, sales promotions, publicity, interactive/social media) • Who does the work on the promotions? (Internal resources or outsourced) • How are promotions paid for? (Partnering, internal compensations)
Price	• Is the product or service price sensitive? • Are there product or service substitutes available? • What research has been done on demand and cost analysis? (Marginal analysis) • Does the product or service have price flexibility? • Are there adjustments to list prices given? (Discounts, allowances)

(Continued)

Table 11.1 (Continued) Marketing OD Consultant Marketing Plan Checklist

People	• What does the internal expertise of employees look like? • What expertise is acquired from outside the organization? (Partners, subcontractors) • What does leadership strength look like? • What capabilities are prevalent within the organization? • What relationship do employees have with customers? • How is the marketing area of the organization structured?
Processes	• What types of total quality management process does the organization utilize? • What type of customer relationship management tool does the organization use? • How does the organization handle strategic planning? • Who is responsible for developing the overall marketing plan and objectives for the organization? • Who is responsible for the oversight of the marketing plan completion? • What types of project management tools are used within the organization? • Who is responsible for product research and development? • How does the organization set an annual marketing budget? • How does the organization view innovation?
Performance	• How does the organization measure and appraise productivity? • How does the organization measure and appraise profitability? • How does the organization build future sales and revenue metrics? • How does the organization measure and expense reduction? • How does the organization monitor, measure, and appraise the completion of the overall annual marketing plan? • How is innovation measured within the organization?
Philosophy	• What is the mission, vision, and core values of the organization? • How closely does the organization live out their mission, vision, and core values? • How does the organization view community involvement? • How does the organization view global awareness? • How does the organization approach strategic planning? • How does the organization approach succession planning?

Defining Measurement and Appraisal

For this chapter, the definition of *measurement* is the act of measuring the outcomes of the interventions. Measuring both the intervention and the outcome variables is necessary to show the overall measurement. Often, in marketing OD, there is a tendency to measure only outcome variables. This tendency is incorrect because an assumption is that since the intervention is implemented, there isn't a need to measure intervention variables. Overall implementation of the intervention takes considerable time, effort, and learning. However, marketing OD consultants must take the time to empirically determine that the intervention has been successfully implemented. Implementation feedback can then guide and help interpret outcome data. If the intervention comprised implementing a new sales training, a negligible change in sales performance could mean several things. This could mean that the wrong intervention was selected, the training program wasn't implemented correctly, or that the wrong variables were measured. This is also the reason intervention variables should derive from the conceptual framework underlying the marketing OD intervention.

The definition of *appraisal* in this chapter is viewed as the act of judging the overall value or importance of the marketing OD intervention to the overall organization goals or bottom-line and whether the intervention has become part of the organization culture. The appraisal step looks closely at whether the behaviors and skill sets gained from the intervention are becoming part of the day-to-day business practice. In OD, this is sometimes referred to as institutionalizing the changes (Cummings & Worley, 2015, p. 221). The Institutionalization Framework includes taking organization characteristics, intervention characteristics, institutionalization processes, and indicators of institutionalization into consideration (p. 222). The organization characteristics include congruence, stability of environment and technology, and unionization (p. 223). Intervention characteristics include goal specificity, programmability, level of change target, internal support, and sponsorship (p. 225). Institutionalization processes include socialization, commitment, reward allocation, diffusion, and sensing and calibration. Indicators of institutionalization include knowledge, performance, preferences, normative consensus, and value consensus (p. 225).

Measurement and appraisal are the processes that make up the final steps of any marketing OD cycle. A marketing OD cycle involves steps that include diagnosis, design, implementation, measurement, and appraisal.

Understanding the measurement and appraisal steps is a critical factor for all clients and consultants to understand and complete.

Importance of Marketing OD Measurement and Appraisal

Executives and organizations investing resources in Marketing OD interventions are being held accountable to show that the intervention was implemented as intended, and that the expected and desired results are being seen. Organization executives must be able to measure the results of the marketing intervention and show how these results link directly to bottom-line outcomes. By appraising the overall intervention, the organization can assess the impact that the intervention is having on an organizational level and that the intervention is becoming part of the day-to-day business practice.

The importance of measurement and appraisal is viewed from different lenses, the consultant lens and the client lens. The consultant uses this step to gauge the success of his performance by looking closely at details and feedback from his clients. This is important so the consultant keeps repetitive business coming from the client or to have the client refer the consultant to additional organizations. The client uses measurement and appraisal techniques to ensure that the intervention has been implemented as planned and that the established outcomes are being seen. By measuring and appraising the intervention, the client can also ensure that a smooth continuation of the effort will take place once the consultant leaves. Finally, the client and the consultant must examine dimensions and processes of the intervention are being accepted or embedded in the day-to-day business practice.

Although these are the main reasons listed over the years why both the consultant and the client would want to complete the steps of marketing measurement and appraisal, additional advantages have been identified, such as the following list:

■ Identifies how the marketing OD intervention meshes into the culture of the organization
■ Measures and compares the marketing program, process, and system effectiveness to intervention effectiveness
■ Facilitates clear communication from the top of the organization and distributes to all stakeholders

- Utilizes measurement and appraisal as a means to high-quality "lessons learned" opportunities by reflecting in a more empirically supported analysis
- Builds an understanding with senior leadership that outcomes measurement and appraisal for marketing OD interventions should be used in measuring the success for leadership within the organization
- Moves the organization towards results-oriented measurement and appraisal
- Builds measurement and appraisal into the organization culture and engage it as a part of ongoing OD.

This expanded list views measurement and appraisal from an overall organizational level. The question could be asked, why don't more organizations look at the overall organizational level when completing the marketing OD measurement and appraisal process? First, some practitioners and consultants may answer this question by stating that when the measurement and appraisal are being looked at from an organizational level, the process becomes too complex because of the many stakeholders involved. This can cause many challenges because of the different interests, interpersonal make up, and organization political agendas. A rebuttal to this shortsightedness could be to express that the importance of operating at the organizational level could increase chances of successful outcomes because of the ability to work directly with those individuals in the organization that have the power to make changes. Second, viewing projects, programs, and interventions in the organizational view could lead the organization to understand that these initiatives may depend on changing the organization of which they are embedded. Lastly, the organization comprises many systems and processes with interdependent parts and changing one system or process could affect other systems and processes and possibly the entire organization. When practitioners and marketing OD consultants view measurement and appraisal at the organizational level, the focus of the marketing OD intervention shifts from intervention effectiveness to organizational effectiveness.

How to Complete Measurement and Appraisal

Marketing OD assessment has historically focused on attitudinal outcomes while overlooking hard measures. For example, some practitioners or marketing OD consultants have measured attitudinal outcomes such as customer satisfaction ratings. However, organizations are now requiring managers and consultants to show how marketing OD interventions are changing and enhancing work-related behaviors that involve producing at work and showing how these results are affecting the bottom-line profit for the organization.

One way to measure and appraise a marketing OD intervention is to look at marketing competencies. Marketing OD consultants can review marketing competencies with their client organizations. This review can help the consultant and client find potential gaps in marketing interventions, strategies, or programs. Several external marketing competencies that can be reviewed are knowledge of customers, knowledge of competitors, and knowledge of industry trends. Several internal marketing competencies to review are awareness of organizational marketing weaknesses, understanding of strategic marketing processes and control, and assessment of marketing activities. These are just a few of the many marketing competencies to consider.

In the past, measurement and appraisal took a more activity-based approach. For example, one of the differences in activity-based approach versus the results-based approach would be how organizations engaged employees in the intervention. In the activity-based approach, the employees were not fully engaged or prepared to participate in the intervention. Activity-based approach is antiquated and can be related more toward the initial four P's of marketing: product, place, price, and promotion. This type of approach is inadequate because it fails to view how people or employees mesh into the overall approach. People is one of the new 8 P's of marketing. Understanding how the people (employees or customers) are engaged with the organization and specifically the intervention is critical to the overall success of the marketing OD intervention. Under the results-based approach, the organization communicates the result expectations continuously to the employees and stakeholders throughout and after the intervention is completed.

Another example would be how the organization is prepared for the intervention. In the activity-based approach, the organization isn't properly prepared to reinforce the implementation of the marketing OD intervention. In the results-based approach, the organization is prepared to reinforce the marketing OD intervention to ensure that the expected and outlined behavior changes happen and these changes impact the organization's bottom-line. Last, under the activity-based approach, organizations usually failed to complete a thorough results or cost–benefit analysis in real tangible

Table 11.2 Behavioral Outcomes Measured in Marketing OD Interventions (Financial Services Industry)

Definition	Categories	Activity Based	Results Based
New customer acquisition:	• Direct • Indirect • Referred	Acquisition issue identified but not captured in a quantifiable and measureable manner	Customer acquisition measured by mode (direct, indirect, and referred), branch, and employee
New customer service satisfaction rating: quality of service given to customer as given in percentage of overall satisfaction.	• Below average • Average • Above average • Best practice	Performance issue identified and rated	Satisfaction rating measured in quantifiable ways to show gap of performance issue vs. expectation and how customer service directly links to bottom-line
New sales productivity and new branches: comparison of sales activity measured in overall sales.	Percentage of total sales increase/ decrease month after month	Measurement of individual sales	Measured in ROI calculation and effect on bottom-line

measurements. In the results-based approach, the thorough results and cost–benefit analysis is completed in the way of showing ROI.

Table 11.2 is a basic table showing the difference between measuring activity-based and results-based approaches.

ROI Methodology

A ROI methodology is a proven approach that the marketing OD consultant or practitioner used to plan, collect, analyze, and communicate outcomes that measure OD projects or interventions. As stated previously in this chapter, the role of measurement and appraisal is crucial for establishing the impact of marketing OD interventions. The role of marketing OD consultants and practitioners is to accept and embrace the understanding that the basis of measurement and appraisal is data driven and therefore leads to using an ROI methodology to show the value of each marketing OD intervention. There are many rational reasons for marketing OD consultants to utilize ROI as an effective measure for OD. Here are just a few.

- Using the language of ROI is speaking the same language as senior leaders and executives.
- Stakeholders are more likely to understand and support the marketing OD intervention if they are shown how the intervention will help the organization's bottom-line.
- Employees are more apt to engage with the intervention or change if they understand how the intervention affects what they do.
- The ability to show a clearer depiction of actual results. ROI measures actual cost input to actual financial impact to the organization.

Why Do Marketing OD Interventions Fail?

When organizations fail to understand the importance of measurement and appraisal, there is a higher rate of failure. Reasons marketing OD interventions fail include consultant or organization lack of understanding of the 8 P's of marketing, lack of business alignment and marketing OD intervention, not preparing the organization for the change management the intervention brings, failure to identify which behavior and impact objectives to measure, lack of understanding organization culture, failure to build data collection plans into the process, and not using the data identified for continual process improvement.

Summary

This chapter provided a basic understanding of measurement and appraisal and the changes with these assessments over the years. Elaboration was given to the changes in terms between evaluation and appraisal and why appraisal takes a more holistic view. Explanation was given on the importance of a marketing OD consultant's understanding of measurement and appraisal. An understanding was given for why measurement and appraisal must be thoroughly understood by both the marketing consultant and the organization in order to ensure a unified agreement to the overall value or success of the marketing intervention. A thorough description of the 8 P's of marketing was provided and elaborated upon in the overall marketing OD consultant checklist. The importance of completing an ROI, which is one way in which to measure the overall success of the marketing OD intervention as well as several metrics for understanding the difference between activity-based and results-based measurement, was provided. A business case scenario was provided to give an example of what a marketing OD consultant or practitioner may ponder before agreeing to complete a marketing OD intervention. The chapter concluded by giving a list of reasons why marketing OD measurement and appraisal may fail was provided.

References

Cummings, T., & Worley, C. (2015). *Organization development & change* (10th ed.). Beaverton: Ringgold.

Kirkpatrick, D., & Kirkpatrick, J. (2006). *Evaluating training program: The four levels* (3rd ed.). San Francisco: Berrett-Koehler Publishers.

Phillips, J.J. (2011). *Return on investment in training and performance improvement programs.* New York: Routledge.

Chapter 12

The Future of Marketing OD Consulting

William J. Rothwell

Contents

Trend 1: OD Consultants Will Grow More Skillful at Using Social Media ... 190
Trend 2: OD Consultants Will Grow More Skillful at Using Word-of-Mouth
Marketing Methods.. 192
Trend 3: OD Consultants Will Improve How They Distinguish
Themselves from Change Management Consultants 192
Trend 4: OD Consultants Will Do More Institutional Marketing 193
Trend 5: OD Consultants Will Improve Their Global Reach 193
Trend 6: OD Marketing Will Expand into Philanthropy............................... 194
Summary 196

What is the future of marketing organization development (OD) consulting? That is the simple, but difficult, question this chapter addresses.

There are trends in marketing. But those are not the same as trends in marketing OD consulting services. This chapter briefly addresses six important trends in marketing OD, pointing the way toward the future. The chapter ends with a tool that invites readers to brainstorm on their own thoughts about these trends, and others, that may influence the future of marketing OD consulting services.

Trend 1: OD Consultants Will Grow More Skillful at Using Social Media

Many people are trying to figure out how to use social media more effectively to conduct marketing. While the age-old approach of word-of-mouth reputation (referrals from one client to others) remains an important way that OD consultants secure business, it is slowly being supplanted by virtual marketing methods. While people will always value interpersonal contact, they are increasingly reliant on virtual methods. Examples of social media include YouTube, Facebook, LinkedIn, Plaxo, and Twitter, and many other social media are just now emerging.

While social media is now all the rage, the problem is there are few real experts knowledgeable about it. The only way to learn it, and get value from social media, is to experiment with it. That means many people are using trial-and-error methods, tracking what works and what does not. Smart people invest more money in doing more of what works and divest doing what does not work.

Consider a few simple examples.

A small-scale interview study with practicing OD consultants revealed that many now secure their business primarily, although not exclusively, by LinkedIn. Savvy OD consultants will slave over their LinkedIn profiles to ensure that they are targeted to reveal just the right key words to ensure that they pop up on the radar screen of anyone who wants to find a consultant capable of leading an OD effort to meet a client-identified need.

YouTube is also a critically important method by which to market OD consulting services. While clients may not be familiar with OD or with a consultant's unique approach to a change intervention, clients can easily relate to a video that demonstrates the change process. Videos are also effective methods by which to collect testimonials from enthusiastically satisfied clients or stakeholders in the change effort. Clients can be asked to discuss what prompted the change effort, how it was carried out, how it differs from other approaches to change that might be used, how the consultant added value to the process, and what results were eventually obtained from using the approach.

Facebook is ubiquitous. While no longer so popular with teenagers who have fled to Snapchat and Instagram, perhaps out of concern that using Facebook might categorize them as like their parents, Facebook has many consulting uses. A consulting firm, or a consultant, can host a Facebook site and use it to foster communication among clients, prospective clients, and those interested in the change intervention that the consultant uses.

Twitter, while limited in the length of content that may be sent out to others, has the advantage of being fast and less intrusive than e-mail or other media. OD consultants may use Twitter to maintain contact with present or prospective future clients. OD consultants may also use Twitter during interventions to keep the change effort uppermost in the minds of those with whom they are consulting.

Webinars are also popular ways to reach many people. Software such as Skype, GoToMeeting, Adobe Connect, or Webex are popular venues by which to present PowerPoint slides and hold discussions with small or large groups of people. Webinars are conducted to educate people on concepts about change; they can present a description of a successful change effort; they can document what is being done and why for future audiences in the same or other organizations; and they can help build important communication channels to keep workers and decision makers attuned to unfolding events across a global organizational change platform. Many professional associations host webinars at no cost or at low cost as a way to foster communication and information sharing among their members. Although marketing may not be obvious (or onerous), it can be subtle in this venue.

OD consultants will make use of virtual reality methods and simulations to give clients and stakeholders the simulated experience of using a change intervention. They can thus "try it out" before they go through it. A simplistic example of virtual reality might be something like Second Life, which has admittedly fallen into some disfavor, but the concept remains intriguing. Each individual in a group can meet in a virtual reality setting—such as a conference room or on an island. They can then interact as they would in the real world; alternatively, they can role play other approaches with interaction. In Second Life, individuals can build their own Avatars, which permits them to try out reality in ways impossible in the real world. For instance, a white person can assume the avatar of a black person in Second Life; a woman can assume the avatar of a man in Second Life. That experience shows people how others react to them based on race, gender, or other characteristics that may not be matched by real-world situations. It can be immensely instructive about how superficial differences among people may change interpersonal interaction.

Trend 2: OD Consultants Will Grow More Skillful at Using Word-of-Mouth Marketing Methods

Word-of-mouth marketing is the oldest approach to marketing OD consulting services. Since the beginning of OD, satisfied clients would share with others their positive experiences with consultants, change efforts, and consequences of change efforts. It could work the other way as well: dissatisfied clients would share with others their negative experiences with consultants, change efforts, and consequences of change efforts. There is nothing new about word-of-mouth marketing except some new labels—such as "establishing a brand identity" (which means nothing more than "set yourself apart from other consultants by getting people to talk about you for what you do well").

But word-of-mouth marketing has new twists and ways of use. One twist is to elevate one-on-one discussions to virtual settings, using social media, where many people can share their experiences. A second twist is to partner with satisfied clients by cobranding and copresenting with them by publishing case studies of successful change efforts, shooting videos about successful change efforts and uploading them, and copresenting case studies at conferences or in webinars. Clients should do that as a communication vehicle to present information inside their own organizations; consultants should do that as a marketing vehicle to convince prospective clients to check them out and consider doing the same thing that another client has found helpful. A third twist is for the consultant to build a track record of successes, and testimonials, that can be shared with a broader audience through social media.

Trend 3: OD Consultants Will Improve How They Distinguish Themselves from Change Management Consultants

Much confusion exists in the world today about the difference between change management and OD. Even experts may disagree on what these terms mean and how the practices of change management consultants may differ from, or overlap with, those of OD consultants.

But matters will sort themselves out. It will become increasingly apparent how change management and OD overlap and how they differ. By clarifying that distinction, practitioners in each field will be better positioned to set themselves apart from their brethren in the other field.

Trend 4: OD Consultants Will Do More Institutional Marketing

Traditionally, OD consultants do not use mass media outlets such as television, radio, or print media like billboards to advertise and market what they do. Advertising as a marketing approach appears to be more common for consumer marketing such as selling televisions, cable services, automobiles, or other products and services that consumers are immediately familiar with. It is not common on OD consulting or in change management consulting.

There are two kinds of advertising. One focuses on a product or service by one organization. When Tide (laundry detergent) presents a commercial on television, the company is promoting a product. A second focuses on an industry, concept, or notion. That is called institutional marketing. When the oil fracking industry presents a commercial on television, all the companies in an entire industry are promoting an idea—that is, that fracking for oil is not harmful to the environment.

There is need for more institutional marketing in OD to educate workers and managers about what OD is, how it works, how it differs from other change approaches, and what benefits can be obtained from it. Institutional marketing could also dispel common sources of resistance to OD—such as the idea it takes too long, is too costly, or uses only "touchy feely" methods that are sentimental and do not make good business sense. By investing in institutional marketing, all OD consultants would gain. The reason: workers and managers would be more aware of what OD is, when to use it, how to use it, and how it contrasts with other change approaches.

Trend 5: OD Consultants Will Improve Their Global Reach

As the world continues to become more globalized, OD consultants must follow suit.

Some years ago, during the financial crisis, I had a conversation with a colleague. He was an OD consultant. I met with him over lunch when I was in Chicago to present at a conference. During our lunchtime conversation, he admitted that his business was suffering greatly due to economic conditions. "I have lost all my clients," he admitted with a look of dismay. Before I asked him why he thought he lost them, I asked him this: "Where is your business coming from? Domestic or foreign?" He answered immediately: "It is all local." My response: "There is your problem. You have restricted your business out of convenience, not wanting to be far from family. But you must follow the business. Most of it is not in the U.S. or Europe but in other growth markets." He got the point.

The same advice illustrates the trend I am discussing. Much OD work is to be done offshore. And many are ripe for picking, so to speak. Many nations do not have universities that train OD consultants, and many managers in developing nations sense the need for OD but cannot precisely explain it in the way a manager from a more sophisticated company or culture could. But the need exists and will only grow in time.

I have had to share some of my own preconceptions along the way. At one time, I doubted if OD methods, relying on trust about the value of everyone's opinions, would work in authoritarian nations or where the workforce was poorly educated and highly inexperienced. I have since rethought those ideas. OD works in those settings, and I have seen it. The challenge is to get the word out, build awareness of OD as a philosophy and an approach, and demonstrate results. In a word, the field faces a marketing challenge. OD is not so much dead as it is less commonly familiar than OD consultants would like to think.

The real challenge is marketing OD globally. How to get the word out? How to explain it to others? How to help them experience its value and possible contributions? These are the questions that must be answered today—and in the future.

Trend 6: OD Marketing Will Expand into Philanthropy

Many business leaders are responding to a social trend whereby investors and members of the public expect organizations of all stripes to be better, more socially responsible corporate citizens. Millennials want to be proud of their organizations for the work they do and how they contribute to the general betterment of humanity. That idea resonates with many OD practitioners.

One approach to marketing that is likely to grow in the future is that OD practitioners will be more likely to step up to leadership roles in philanthropical activities—such as social causes, charities, and nonprofit work.

Donating time and services to build a positive brand identity is a future trend that will affect OD. OD consultants in the future will seek out social issues, try to assume leadership roles, and demonstrate how OD can contribute to the betterment of humanity. While that is an effort worthy to do in its own right, it is also a marketing strategy that will demonstrate how OD works to those unfamiliar with it.

Table 12.1   A Worksheet for Trends in Marketing OD

Directions: Use this Worksheet to do some brainstorming and to structure and organize your own thinking about how to address future trends affecting OD marketing. For each trend listed in the left column below, brainstorm some thoughts in the right column about how you can address the trend at present and in the future. In the last items in the left column, add some of your own opinions about future trends affecting OD marketing and then offer your own thoughts in the right column about how to address those trends. There are no right or wrong answers to this activity in any absolute sense, but some ideas may be better than others. The better your ideas, the more effectively you should be able to market OD consulting services in the future.

Trends in Marketing OD		*Brainstorm Your Own Ideas About What to Do*
1	OD consultants will grow more skillful at using social media	
2	OD consultants will grow more skillful at using word-of-mouth marketing methods	
3	OD consultants will improve how they distinguish themselves from change management consultants	
4	OD consultants will do more institutional marketing	
5	OD consultants will improve their global reach	
6	OD marketing will expand into philanthropy	
7	Other trends (*List them below and then provide your answers under the right column.*)	

Summary

This chapter listed six possible future trends affecting OD marketing. First, OD consultants will grow more skillful at using social media. Second, OD consultants will grow more skillful at using word-of-mouth marketing methods. Third, OD consultants will improve how they distinguish themselves from change management consultants. Fourth, OD consultants will do more institutional marketing. Fifth, OD consultants will improve their global reach. And sixth and finally, OD marketing will expand into philanthropy. Use the worksheet appearing in Table 12.1 to brainstorm on your own thoughts about your own future marketing efforts for OD.

Index

A

Action Research Model (ARM), 7, 53
Active listening, 109
Aspirant company, 139

B

Behavioral outcomes, 185t
Blogs, 104, 110, 111, 145
Branding concept, 130
Business case studies (communication),
    161–163

C

Capability statement, 46–49
    core competencies, 47
    corporate data, 47
    definition, 46
    differentiators, 47
    factors, 47
    importance of, 46
    modification, 49
    organization overview, 47
    past performances, 47
    sample, 48
    types, 46–47
CBD, *see* Commerce Business Daily
Change management, performance
    consulting, and organization
    development (unique challenges
    in marketing), 1–11

Action Research Model, 7
    description of change management, 2–3
    description of OD, 6–8
    description of performance consulting, 3–5
    importance of marketing, 9–10
    models, 2
    unsought good, 9
    what change management, performance
        consulting, and OD share in
        common, 8
    worksheet, 11t
C-level executives, methods of accessing,
    163–168
    build networks with linchpins within the
        organization, 165–166
    climb up the authorized ladder, 163–165
    improve credibility and visibility, 166–168
    media exposure, 167
    viral marketing, 165
    worksheet, 168t
Client management, 155–156
Commerce Business Daily (CBD), 72
Communication planning and branding,
    123–131
    branding concept, 130
    case study, 124
    communication aligned with branding,
        124–125
    communication comes first, 125
    communication tools for internal OD
        professional, 129
    expertise meets target market, 125

first meeting, 127–129
keeping in touch, 129
keys to communication, 125–127
OD interventions, 126t
protecting the brand, 130–131
referrals, 130
Communications, executive-level,
    see Executive-level
    communications
Competencies, *see* Personal strengths
    and weaknesses, evaluation of
    (competency-based approach)
"Cost of doing business," 83
Customer
    -driven marketing strategy, 24–25
    equity, 28
    needs and wants, 23–24
    relationship groups 29t
    satisfaction, 17
    testimonials, 20

D

Definitions
    capability statement, 46
    competency, 32
    marketing defined, 15–16
    measurement and appraisal, 181–182
    self-promotion 144
    WOM marketing 116

E

Elevator pitch, 135, 143f
Executive-level communications, 159–172
    business case studies, 161–163
        approaching C-level executives to
            market your service, 161–163
        case discussion, 163
    C-level executives, methods of accessing,
        163–168
        build networks with linchpins within
            the organization, 165–166
        climb up the authorized ladder,
            163–165
        improve credibility and visibility,
            166–168

media exposure, 167
viral marketing, 165
worksheet, 168t
differences between internal and
    external OD consultants, 161, 162t
tips, 168–172
    difference between OD consulting and
        management consulting, 169
    focus on what C-level executives are
        interested in, 170
    keep your communication simple,
        171–172
    make opportunities for continuous
        communication, 171
    persuade them on even ground,
        170–171
    remind them that OD is their
        responsibility, 169

F

Facebook, 110, 111–112, 146
Feedback, 62, 93, 181
Four I's of services, 18
Four Levels of Evaluation Model
    (Kirkpatrick), 176
Four P's, 177
Franchises, 58
Future of marketing OD consulting (trends),
    189–196
    change management consultants,
        distinguishing from, 192–193
    global reach, 193–194
    institutional marketing, 193
    philanthropy, 194–195
    social media, 190–191
    word-of-mouth marketing methods, 192
    worksheet, 195t

G

Global reach, 193–194
Government RFPs, 76

H

Huffington Post, 146

I

Instagram, 110, 113
Institutional marketing, 193
Invitation for bid, 74

J

Journal submissions, 147

K

Key terms, 14t

L

Leading questions, 109
LinkedIn, 104, 110, 113, 146

M

Marketing channels, 103–121
    case study, 117–119
    social media, 110–115
        activity, 114–115
        blogs, 111
        Facebook, 111–112
        Instagram, 113
        LinkedIn, 113
        social networking, 111–114
        Twitter, 113–114
        WhatsApp, 112–113
        YouTube, 110
    social networking and referrals, 108–109
        active listening, 109
        follow-up, 109
        question-asking skills, 109
    strategies, 105–108
        charity goodwill, 108
        marketing at professional conferences,
            106–107
        mission statement and branding, 105
        professional associations and events,
            105–106
        publications, 107
    WOM marketing, 115–117
        activity, 116–117

    definition, 116
    negative, 116
Marketing landscape, tools, and definitions,
    13–30
    key terms 14t
    marketing overview, 15–18
        building strong relationships with
            customers, 17–18
        capturing value in return from
            customers, 18
        creating value for customers, 17
        customer satisfaction, 17
        marketing defined, 15–16
        stages of marketing, 16f, 16t
        target market, 15
    marketing process, 22–29
        customer relationship groups, 29t
        step 1 (understand the marketplace and
            customer needs and wants), 23–24
        step 2 (design a customer-driven
            marketing strategy), 24–25
        step 3 (construct an integrated
            marketing program that delivers
            superior value), 25–26
        step 4 (build profitable relationships
            and create customer delight), 27–28
        step 5 (capture value from customers
            to create profits and customer
            equity), 28
    OD consultant, marketing services for,
        18–22
        customer testimonials, 20
        four I's of services, 18
        inconsistency, 21
        inseparability, 21–22
        intangibility, 19–21
        inventory, 22
Measurement and appraisal, relevance of,
    173–187
    aspects to consider as a marketing OD
        consultant, 177–180
        four P's, 177
        marketing plan checklist, 178t–180t
    defining measurement and appraisal,
        181–182
    Four Levels of Evaluation Model
        (Kirkpatrick), 176

historical perspective, 176–177
how to complete measurement and
    appraisal, 183–185
    activity-based approach, 184
    behavioral outcomes, 185t
    marketing competencies, 184
    preparation for intervention, 184
importance of marketing OD
    measurement and appraisal, 182–183
marketing OD business case scenario,
    174–176
ROI methodology, 185–186
V-Model (Phillip), 176
why marketing OD interventions fail, 186
Memorandum of agreement (MOA), 94

N

Negative WOM marketing, 116
Niche consulting practice, creation of, 53–54
Niche market identification, 54–60
    determining strengths, 58–60
    franchises, 58
    parameter-based niche consulting, 55–56
    pitfalls of niche marketing, 57–58
    protective barriers, 57
    success factors in niche marketing, 56–57
Nongovernment RFPs, 76

O

Organization development (OD), 1, *see also*
    Change management, performance
    consulting, and organization
    development (unique challenges in
    marketing)
    consultant, competencies for, 32–34
    consultant, marketing services for, 18–22
        customer testimonials, 20
        inconsistency, 21
        inseparability, 21–22
        intangibility, 19–21
        inventory, 22
    consulting services, *see* Pricing of OD
        consulting services
    description of, 6–8
Organization Development Network, 33

P

Performance consulting, *see* Change
    management, performance
    consulting, and organization
    development (unique challenges
    in marketing)
Personal sales, 133–157
    client management, 155–156
    critical questions, 134–144
        How are you going to earn income?,
        142–144
        What is your product?, 135–136
        What makes your services different?,
        140–141
        Who are you competing against?,
        139–140
        Who are your customers/clients?,
        136–137
        Who are your main stakeholders?,
        137–138
    presentations, 147–154
        call to action, 151
        components, 148
        content, 149–152
        delivery, 153–154
        information, 150
        introduction, 150
        medium, 152
        structure, 148–149
    proposal writing, 154–155
    self-promotion, 144–147
        blogging sites, 145
        definition, 144
        journal submissions, 147
        traditional ways of, 144
        US Postal Service, 147
        website development, 145
Personal strengths and weaknesses,
    evaluation of (competency-based
    approach), 31–50
    capability statement, 46–49
        core competencies, 47
        corporate data, 47
        definition, 46
        differentiators, 47
        factors, 47

importance of, 46
modification, 49
organization overview, 47
past performances, 47
sample, 48
types, 46–47
consulting styles of OD consultants,
34–46
identification of style, 40
roles and responsibilities, 41–45
OD consultants, competencies for, 32–34
definition of competency, 32
Organization Development Network,
33
participative change efforts, 32
survey, 33
worksheet, 35t–39t
Presentations, 147–154
call to action, 151
components, 148
content, 149–152
delivery, 153–154
information, 150
introduction, 150
medium, 152
structure, 148–149
Pricing of OD consulting services, 91–102
common pricing situations, 92–94
difference from pricing other consulting,
95–96
memorandum of agreement, 94
philosophical issues, 96–100
client-based rate, 98
combination, 99
consistency-based rate, 99
consultant-based rate, 97
creative approaches to rates, 100
market-based rate, 97
place-based rate, 98
targeted rate, 96–97
value-based rate, 99
work-based rate, 98
return on investment, 94
worksheet, 101
Proposal process, 71–89
clarifying your role, 78–80
consultant, 78–80

contractor, 78
freelancer, 78
management consulting, 80
OD consulting, 79–80
financial terms and conditions, 82–86
budget narrative, 82
"cost of doing business," 83
costs, 83
worksheet, 83t–85t
proposal template 87t–89t
proposal writing, 80–82
goals and objectives, 80
proposal elements, 82
proposal evaluation scoring
worksheet, 81
request for proposal, 72–77
closed, 73
government RFPs, 76
internal vs. external solicited request,
74–75
invitation for bid, 74
nongovernment RFPs, 76
process, 73f
sole source invitation, 73
solicited request, 73–76, 75f
unsolicited request, 76–77
target audience, 77

Q

Question-asking skills, 109

R

Relationship marketing, tips for, 57
Request for proposal (RFP), 48, 72–77
closed, 73
government RFPs, 76
internal vs. external solicited request,
74–75
invitation for bid, 74
nongovernment RFPs, 76
process, 73f
sole source invitation, 73
solicited request, 73–76, 75f
unsolicited request, 76–77
Request for quotation (RFQ), 74

Request for tender (RFT), 74
Return on investment (ROI), 94, 185–186

S

Self-promotion, 144–147
  blogging sites, 145
  definition, 144
  journal submissions, 147
  traditional ways of, 144
  US Postal Service, 147
  website development, 145
Social media, 104, 110–115
  activity, 114–115
  blogs, 111
  Facebook, 111–112
  Instagram, 113
  LinkedIn, 113
  social networking, 111–114
  trends, 190–191
  Twitter, 113–114
  WhatsApp, 112–113
  YouTube, 110
Sole source invitation, 73
SWOT analysis, 178

T

Target market, 15
Trends, *see* Future of marketing OD
      consulting (trends)
Twitter, 104, 110, 113–114

U

Unmet needs and opportunities, evaluation
    of, 51–70
  business case study, 53–54
    action research model, 53
    creating a parameter-based niche
      consulting practice, 53–54
  feedback, 62
  niche market identification, 54–60
    determining strengths, 58–60

  parameter-based niche consulting,
      55–56
  pitfalls of niche marketing, 57–58
  protective barriers, 57
  success factors in niche marketing,
      56–57
personal branding for niche consulting in
    OD, 61–62
relationship marketing, tips for, 57
strategy development, 63–69
  entrepreneurial marketing strategies, 66
  market analysis and evaluation, 63–64
  niche marketing strategies, 66–67
  value proposition development, 64–65
  why marketing plans are overlooked,
      68–69
  worksheet, 67–68
Unsought good, 9
US Postal Service, 147

V

Viral marketing, 165
V-Model (Phillip), 176

W

Website development, 145
Weekly Standard, The, 146
WhatsApp, 110, 112–113
Word-of-mouth (WOM) marketing, 104,
      115–117
  activity, 116–117
  definition, 116
  methods, 192
  negative, 116

X

XYZ competency study, 48

Y

YouTube, 110